Making Sense of the Dollars:
The Costs and Uses of Faculty Compensation

by Kathryn M. Moore and Marilyn J. Amey

ASHE-ERIC Higher Education Report No. 5, 1993

Prepared by

Clearinghouse on Higher Education
The George Washington University

In cooperation with

ASHE

Association for the Study
of Higher Education

Published by

School of Education and Human Development
The George Washington University

Jonathan D. Fife, Series Editor

Cite as
Moore, Kathryn M., and Marilyn J. Amey. 1993. *Making Sense of the Dollars: The Costs and Uses of Faculty Compensation.* ASHE-ERIC Higher Education Report No. 5. Washington, D.C.: The George Washington University, School of Education and Human Development.

Library of Congress Catalog Card Number 93-61675
ISSN 0884-0040
ISBN 1-878380-26-5

Managing Editor: Bryan Hollister
Manuscript Editor: Barbara Fishel, Editech
Cover design by Michael David Brown, Rockville, Maryland

The ERIC Clearinghouse on Higher Education invites individuals to submit proposals for writing monographs for the *ASHE-ERIC Higher Education Report* series. Proposals must include:
1. A detailed manuscript proposal of not more than five pages.
2. A chapter-by-chapter outline.
3. A 75-word summary to be used by several review committees for the initial screening and rating of each proposal.
4. A vita and a writing sample.

ERIC Clearinghouse on Higher Education
School of Education and Human Development
The George Washington University
One Dupont Circle, Suite 630
Washington, DC 20036-1183

This publication was prepared partially with funding from the Office of Educational Research and Improvement, U.S. Department of Education, under contract no. ED RI-88-062014. The opinions expressed in this report do not necessarily reflect the positions or policies of OERI or the Department.

EXECUTIVE SUMMARY

The well-being of the professoriat depends on a solid financial foundation in institutions of higher education. Simply put, unless adequate remuneration is available, talented individuals will seek other employment—both faculty who are currently in the professoriat and those who might be recruited to undergo the preparation and enter the professoriat subsequently.

During the 1970s and 1980s, faculty salaries declined sharply, in both real and relative comparisons, and the decline was combined with a widening dispersion of salaries across disciplines. It has resulted in a variety of inequities and discontinuities for individuals and for institutions. In light of an increasingly dynamic job market for faculty in the 1990s, it is important that both faculty and institutional decision makers understand what is involved in compensation policies and practices to improve and preserve the professoriat and the higher education enterprise it serves.

What Is the Current Context?

The current context for decisions concerning compensation is extremely turbulent. The financial situation of many states has reached crisis levels. Public higher education is under duress. Many institutions have had to make deep cuts in their budgets—as much as 15 to 20 percent—and no relief is in sight. Because personnel costs amount to approximately 80 percent of most institutions' operating budgets, there is virtually no way the faculty can be sheltered from such cuts.

In addition, today's faculty are far more diverse, certainly more sophisticated about the marketplace, and more informed of the general state of affairs affecting their institutions and the professoriat generally than were their earlier counterparts. In return for their contributions, they expect institutional leaders to provide wise policy, humane practice, and dedicated service in return. Compensation policy and practice are at the center of an institution's relationship with its faculty. Indeed, compensation policy and practice reflect the essential mission and philosophy of each institution through what it rewards, whom it rewards, and how it treats its most important human resource.

How Is Compensation Structured?

Compensation usually refers to salary plus other monetary payments or quasi-monetary payments, such as fringe benefits.

It might also include nonmonetary compensation like leaves of absence, released time, and sometimes even laboratory or other work space. Most depictions of faculty compensation tend to focus exclusively on the salary portion. *Making Sense of the Dollars: The Costs and Uses of Faculty Compensation* takes a more comprehensive approach, however, examining the structure of compensation and key decision points involved in determining institutionally appropriate structures of compensation, including linking compensation to institutional mission. While not a factor at every institution, collective bargaining agreements play important roles when they do exist. Retirement issues and their impact on the structure of compensation, including early retirement programs and incentives, are important also.

How Do the Academic Labor Market and Other Factors Affect Compensation?

Recent federal legislation uncapping retirement has called attention to the age structure of the academic work force and indirectly to how faculty are remunerated. Projections for the academic work force for 2000 make two principal observations: (1) Senior levels of faculty will be reduced as much as 40 percent because of retirements; and (2) replacements for these departing scholars are not entirely evident.

The overarching perspective is one that considers institutions as markets and the ability of various types of institutions to preserve and protect their mission and direction through practices of hiring and compensation. External market issues affect institutional polices and practices regarding compensation, including dimensions of the current and prospective faculty labor pools and the dispersion of salaries across academic and nonacademic markets. Internal market issues include the role of faculty as independent professionals within a multidisciplinary market and new contractual and compensatory arrangements for faculty, including retirement.

How Is Compensation Used?

Institutional quality is inextricably bound to the quality of the faculty, yet hiring and retaining high-quality faculty members are likely to become increasingly difficult in the years ahead. Does compensation motivate faculty? What is the rationale behind using merit pay to reward productivity, and are teaching, research, and service rewarded differently?

How is compensation used to reward seniority, and what compensation practices reward faculty activity across the career span? How is compensation used to enhance recruitment and retention, and what institutional issues are associated with the use of supplemental compensation? *Making Sense of the Dollars* examines these questions and provides some answers for faculty and administrators.

Are Faculty Paid Fairly?

Equity is a central concept in pay systems generally. Inequitable policies and practices of compensation can result in poor use of human resources, individual frustration and discord, and lower institutional productivity.

Compensation policy and practice are underwritten by several important federal laws and regulations, and state statutes. The Equal Pay Act of 1963 and Title VII of the Civil Rights Act of 1964 are particularly defining. Considerable controversy surrounds the idea of equity and its application to various individuals and groups within higher education. Claims of salary discrimination have played a crucial role in shaping the nature of the debate since these federal laws were passed. Considerable research has focused on three aspects of salary discrimination: studies that document the existence of salary discrimination; studies that attempt to explain or examine the causes of salary inequity; and research concerning various methodological tools used to prove or disprove salary discrimination nationally and on campus.

How Can We Build Effective Compensation Systems?

Academic compensation has evolved piecemeal in response to changing markets, individual expectations and behaviors, and institutional circumstances. It is a highly complex system that nevertheless strives to achieve a reasonable balance between the faculty's personal and professional needs and a college's or university's mission, goals, and resources. A set of policy dimensions forms the foundation of most collegiate compensation systems. These policies address internal consistency, external competitiveness, individual contributions, and the way the system of compensation is administered.

Increasing external pressure for colleges and universities to be accountable and open in their operations will sooner or later affect their compensation systems. While many institutions have open salary information, others do not. Some have clearly written policies and procedures; others do not. In the long run, the productivity and satisfaction of the faculty—indeed, the overall quality of the institution—will depend on its compensation system and the wisdom with which it is administered.

ADVISORY BOARD

CONSULTING EDITORS

Louis C. Attinasi, Jr.
University of Houston

David W. Breneman
Harvard University

Kimberly Brown
Portland State University

J. Kent Caruthers
MGT of America, Inc.

Elsa Kircher Cole
The University of Michigan

Jane F. Earley
Mankato State University

Walter H. Gmelch
Washington State University

James O. Hammons
University of Arkansas

Robert M. Hendrickson
The Pennsylvania State University

George D. Kuh
Indiana University

Barbara A. Lee
Rutgers University

James L. Morrison
The University of North Carolina-Chapel Hill

Patricia H. Murrell
Memphis State University

Amaury Nora
University of Illinois-Chicago

Robert M. O'Neil
University of Virginia

Raymond V. Padilla
Arizona State University

Barbara S. Plakens
Iowa State University

William Rittenberg
Michigan State University

G. Jeremiah Ryan
Harford Community College

Karen Spear
Fort Lewis College

Kala Stroop
Southeast Missouri State University

John M. Swales
The University of Michigan

Ellen Switkes
University of California–Oakland

Jo Taylor
Wayne State University

William G. Tierney
The Pennsylvania State University

Kathryn Towns
The Pennsylvania State University–Harrisburg

Caroline Turner
University of Minnesota–Twin Cities

Elizabeth A. Williams
University of Massachuetts–Amherst

Richard A. Yanikoski
DePaul University

REVIEW PANEL

Charles Adams
University of Massachusetts–Amherst

Louis Albert
American Association for Higher Education

Richard Alfred
University of Michigan

Philip G. Altbach
State University of New York–Buffalo

Marilyn J. Amey
University of Kansas

Louis C. Attinasi, Jr.
University of Houston

Robert J. Barak
Iowa State Board of Regents

Alan Bayer
Virginia Polytechnic Institute and State University

John P. Bean
Indiana University

John M. Braxton
Vanderbilt University

Peter McE. Buchanan
Council for Advancement and
    Support of Education

John A. Centra
Syracuse University

Arthur W. Chickering
George Mason University

Shirley M. Clark
Oregon State System of Higher Education

Darrel A. Clowes
Virginia Polytechnic Institute and State University

John W. Creswell
University of Nebraska–Lincoln

Deborah DiCroce
Piedmont Virginia Community College

Richard Duran
University of California

CONTENTS

FOREWORD

In a recent ASHE-ERIC Higher Education Report, *Faculty Job Satisfaction: Women and Minorities in Peril,* Martha Tack and Carol Pattitu summarize their findings on salaries:

Major factors in the workplace for faculty members in higher education include salary, tenure, rank, supervision, interpersonal relationships, working conditions, policies and administration, person-environment fit, and collective bargaining. Not surprisingly, salary appears to be one of the greatest sources of dissatisfaction with one's job (1992, pp. 31–32).

It is of little wonder that faculty are dissatisfied with their salaries and general compensation, for most institutions have no comprehensive philosophy or strategy that governs how compensation is determined. Normally, four general considerations apply: (1) How much money is in the budget? (2) How little needs to be paid to get the candidate? (These two considerations are the most important.) (3) Do the salaries compare favorably with the institution's "market basket" or competing institutions? (4) Do the average compensation figures compare favorably with the national norms, such as the annual AAUP salary data? The problem with the last approach is that, even if the institution's average compensation is in line with the national norm, individual compensation packages could be drastically dissimilar. And the results could be dissatisfaction among faculty, low moral, and the ever-present reality of litigation.

If compensation packages are seen as one factor that represents an institution's basic values and directly influences how well the institution functions, not as an individual matter, then the importance of developing a comprehensive compensation philosophy should become more obvious. Basically, how a person is compensated is a statement of how much that person is appreciated and esteemed in relation to all other individuals in the organization. The acceptability of the argument that one academic specialty needs to be paid more than another to attract candidates to the faculty fails when contrasted to the economic or financial value of each faculty member to the institution. When two faculty members teach the same number of students (bring into the institution the same tuition revenue) or have the same amount of funded research, they are adding the same value to the institution and therefore deserve the same compensation.

One significant result in failing to have an institutionwide compensation policy is the potential for discrimination. The situation is usually caused by a candidate's initial bargaining power. But the long-term consequences of offering a lower starting salary to those with less bargaining power are that, over one's career, this inequity is rarely adjusted and greater discrepancies develop.

What factors might be considered in developing compensation policy is the subject of *Making Sense of the Dollars: The Costs and Uses of Faculty Compensation.* Kathryn M. Moore, professor and chair of the Department of Educational Administration at Michigan State University, and Marilyn J. Amey, assistant professor of higher education administration in the Department of Educational Policy and Leadership at the University of Kansas, analyze the major literature and practices concerning the costs and uses of faculty compensation. They first review the general structure that makes up faculty compensation and then examine the reasoning that historically has been used to justify various levels of and programs for compensation. With this background, they then look at the uses of compensation and the equity of faculty compensation. Moore and Amey conclude the report with recommendations for building effective compensation systems.

Salary alone does not act as a long-term motivator. Salaries that are perceived as being unfair, however, lead to long-term dissatisfaction and can have a great impact on the faculty's morale and effectiveness. A carefully constructed compensation system can combine features that will create an atmosphere of fairness and appreciation, the two conditions that research has shown to create the healthiest and most productive workplace. Creating such a system after years of favoritism and systematic neglect is not easy, but increasingly it is a necessity.

Jonathan D. Fife
Series Editor, Professor of Higher Education Administration, and Director, ERIC Clearinghouse on Higher Education

ACKNOWLEDGMENTS

We began work on this topic a number of years ago, beginning with an interest in equity in pay. We wrote it to satisfy
our own need to have a basic understanding of this essential
topic. Often, however, what appear to be simple tasks develop
into complicated activities. Trying to accurately portray issues
related to faculty compensation has proven to be not only
a complicated endeavor, but also has seemed much like chas-
ing a moving train.

We are indebted to many individuals on several campuses,
including the faculty and staff of the Center for the Study of
Higher Education at Penn State University, where we began
our inquiry. Dr. James Fairweather has been consistently helpful and supportive throughout. At Michigan State University,
David Braskamp and Joe Brocato provided indispensable
research assistance, and Barbara Reeves and especially Verla
Ensign provided secretarial support far beyond the norm.

We benefited from conversations with faculty and administrators across the country, particularly those who attended
workshops conducted at AAHE by Kathryn Moore and James
Fairweather. The anonymous reviewers for the monograph
provided useful insights and suggestions on how this monograph could be improved. Finally, we wish to salute our colleagues across the country whose continued scholarly efforts
will provide the means by which we can understand the intricacies of faculty compensation policies and practices in the
future.

THE STRUCTURE OF COMPENSATION

One of the authors' most important themes is the need for more effective compensation policies and practices to better serve the needs of today's collegiate institutions and faculty. Yet the literature lacks clarity and consistency in definitions of, uses of, and meanings associated with compensation. While a "customized" approach to idiosyncratic compensation policies and practices has some validity, several concepts and considerations also pertain regardless of institutional type or mission, including how compensation is structured, what affects the structure, and how compensation is used. Unpacking these fundamentals is the focus of the first sections of this monograph.

Compensation usually refers to salary plus other monetary payments or quasi-monetary payments, such as fringe benefits. It might also include nonfinancial components, such as leaves of absence, released time, and sometimes even laboratory or other work spaces. Most depictions of faculty compensation tend to focus exclusively on salary, and, indeed, for some analyses salary alone is appropriate. This monograph, however, uses a more comprehensive approach to compensation.

Monetary and Quasi-monetary Forms of Compensation

A comprehensive definition of compensation begins with those components referred to as "monetary" and "quasi-monetary," commonly called salary and benefits. Base salary, as the name implies, is that amount of pay from which other elements of monetary and quasi-monetary compensation are derived. Most often, deans or search committees have established salary ranges on which they will negotiate a base salary with the prospective employee. This range is determined by a variety of factors, including rank of the open position and the candidate's years of previous experience. The range can be particularly important in establishing base salaries for associate or full professors, but it can also be a consideration for assistant professors, especially if they have been employed in nontraditional settings, such as independent research laboratories, foundations, business, or government. Various external and internal considerations of the labor market also play a role in determining base salary (see the subsection entitled "The Academic Labor Market" in the next section for a detailed discussion). Comparing starting salaries with similar or regionally competitive institutions and with certain organizations in the private sector often provides an institution

Base salary is that amount of pay from which other elements of monetary and quasi-monetary compensation are derived.

with the same kind of relevant information about compensation candidates seek.

Internally, starting salaries of others in a given department or school are important benchmarks for determining base salaries of new employees and for trying to mitigate salary compression (the narrowed distribution of intra- and interrank salaries). Ranges might also be determined by how much money is available in a given salary line. For instance, if a full professor retires, enough money might be available in the line to fill the position with an assistant professor or an associate professor, whereas if an assistant professor leaves, less money would be available in the line, regardless of academic need. The importance of the factors involved in setting base salary should not be understated. Base salary lays the foundation for compensation packages in general, and the criteria used in determining it could be very telling artifacts of the institution's philosophy toward, and uses of, faculty compensation.

Fringe Benefits
Fringe benefits (indirect compensation) are supplemental to and calculated on base salary, usually ranging from 5 to 40 percent of base salary per benefit category (Bowen 1979; Keister and Keister 1989). In 1943, for example, overall employee benefits averaged less than 5 percent of base salaries; in 1990, the average was 20 percent (McCaffery 1992). Benefits are often more susceptible to extra-academic economic influences than base salaries, however.

Many categories of benefits, varying by kind of institution-wide arrangements, are available to faculty and staff. Many of the fringe benefits that quickly come to mind are those called "protection programs" (McCaffery 1992), which in general include health care (physician and dental services, hospitalization, and so on), disability benefits, life insurance, workers' compensation, unemployment compensation, social security benefits, and institutional contributions to pension funds. Many of these fringe benefits require the employee to share their cost with the institution; other programs might cover the cost for the employee but ask the employee to pay for the family's share of the benefit (Calais 1991). On average, one can expect benefits to account for at least 25 percent of total payroll costs today (Calais 1991), but the percentage could be as high as 35 to 50 percent at larger institutions

(Lawler 1990). In either case, a significant portion of the benefits goes to cover medical expenses (Hamermesh and Woodbury 1991), and as the cost of health care and other services increases, the percentage required to cover benefits will rise as well. We have already seen higher deductibles and "redesigned" benefit packages (Lohmann 1991) in efforts to counteract substantial increases in insurance rates. The portion of benefit dollars allocated to medical-related costs and to retirement/pension costs is growing increasingly disparate (Hamermesh and Woodbury 1991; Lohmann 1991).

A second category of fringe benefits involves pay for time not worked (McCaffery 1992)—sick leave, personal absences, and vacations and holidays, for example, although many probably do not think of these "arrangements" as compensation benefits. Other examples of pay for time not worked for faculty include sabbatical leaves, attendance at conferences, professional development activities, and consulting. From faculty's perspective, they might also not be seen as part of a compensation package, yet the institution incurs certain costs, which must be accounted for in comprehensive compensation planning.

A third category of fringe benefits, "employee services and perquisites," includes employee discounts, educational assistance, and child care (McCaffery 1992). The dollar value of these perquisites for faculty as well as the portion of an employee's contribution to the overall benefit cost vary across institutions. Many of these services are most useful in their demonstrating institutional commitment to overall faculty and staff well-being than in their actual return on capital investment. Even so, their importance continues to increase as the demand for various kinds of employee assistance grows.

Another aspect of compensation is the components of salary that do not fall neatly into any prescribed category. Many elements of compensation that are not tied directly to base salary are still negotiated during the hiring process, at the same time base salary is established. For newly hired faculty members, compensation packages might include "one-time" awards for computer hardware or moving expenses. For many, summer salaries for teaching and/or research are important negotiations that could affect one's ultimate decision to accept a position. Again, as a function of mission and discipline leading to a difference in actual job responsibilities, faculty at research universities might negotiate laboratory facilities, laboratory start-up costs, and graduate research assistants or technicians as part of their initial compensation packages. Conversely, at teaching-oriented universities and colleges, faculty might negotiate for teaching assistants or released time to plan curriculum.

Other kinds of benefits might be available to faculty, although they are not necessarily negotiated at hiring—educational assistance in the form of tuition aid or benefits for spouse or children, for example. Relocation assistance might be available in the form of moving expenses, temporary living expenses, and allowances or loans for purchasing a house. Many institutions now have prepaid legal services or financial planning programs.

Changes in benefit packages
Recent analysts argue that employee benefits is the issue of greatest importance to human resource professionals both inside and outside academe. On the positive side, increased costs and externally initiated changes have resulted in reappraisals of existing benefit packages and service deliverers. From such assessments have come "cafeteria-style" or flexible benefit arrangements, allowing employees to become involved only in those fringe benefits that are personally appropriate for them while not precluding the development of a set of core benefits (Burgess 1985; McCaffery 1992; Silander 1983; Strategic Study Group 1988). Although they are criticized as more expensive to administer, flexible benefit programs appear to increase employees' satisfaction with available benefits. They also allow colleges and universities to match benefit packages offered in the private sector, where flexible benefit programs are becoming more the norm (Haslinger 1985; Heller 1986). Competition among service providers has increased as colleges and universities look for the most value for their compensation dollar. Officers in charge of benefit programs have become more critical assessors of participation in specific programs as well, eliminating those with little or no involvement or shifting the costs entirely to employees (Calais 1991). Efforts to reform health care could provide institutions with greater flexibility in providing options for benefits. Conversely, the process of reform could also require more responsibility for costs shifted to employees as the choice of health care providers becomes more narrow and institutional compensation dollars more restrictive.

Changes in the academic labor market have had a subsequent effect on the type and amount of benefits faculty desire. Comparable changes in the benefits available and to whom and at what cost have not occurred as quickly, although cafeteria-style service delivery could prove to be a useful vehicle to deliver benefits. For example, the growing number of women and single parents in the work force adds the concern of adequate child care to the list of benefits desired. Often, on-site day care is made available to faculty to resolve the need (Kraft 1984). An alternative strategy is to allow for adequate tax-deferred contributions to off-site day care programs (Univ. of Kansas 1991). Other benefits include tax-favored, dependent-care reimbursement accounts, child care resource and referral services, family or parental leaves, elder care, and adoption benefits. Following the private sector's slow lead, colleges and universities are making headway in addressing this increasing need. Without appropriate benefits and administrative support for child care and other emerging needs, some believe the risk of higher faculty turnover increases substantially, especially among women (Moore and Johnson 1989).

Faculty need extended maternity and parental leaves for meeting familial care responsibilities more today than in decades past. The University of Michigan, for example, has instituted a program of family care initiatives designed to address the needs of its faculty. Included in the program are childbearing and dependent-care leave programs, a "modified duties" policy that provides leave from teaching based on the effects of pregnancy, childbirth, or related medical conditions without penalty to the faculty member, and a family-care resources program that assists in locating suitable care arrangements or similar resources for family members of faculty and staff (Hollenshead 1992). The family-care program, particularly those aspects related to leave without penalty, is in part an attempt to provide benefits faculty had in theory but not in practice. Certainly changes in benefit programs entail associated costs, yet the administration and faculty at the University of Michigan feel the economic costs are worth the contribution to faculty recruitment and retention.

The growing prevalence of dual-career couples is another change in the labor market that challenges traditionally designed benefit plans. More and more campuses seek to assist in placing spouses or partners in jobs, both on and off campus. Spousal benefits for the partners of gay men and lesbians and nonmarried heterosexual partners that are normally provided for husbands and wives are also requested on some campuses (D'Emilio 1990). One challenge of the 1990s is the development of sound, inclusive compensation policies that reflect the range of existing and prospective faculty life and career orientations (a variety of issues affecting equity are addressed later).

The overall relationship of salary and benefits

The relationship between base salary and benefits has been assumed to be positive. In restrictive financial times, however, critics warn that the relationship might need to be reevaluated. According to some analyses, it might no longer be fiscally responsible to assume regular annual increases in both salary and benefits (Calais 1991). Policy planners might need to consider separating benefits from salary in terms of costs to employers or employees and annual increases. For instance, the promise of tuition benefits for children ten years in the future might be less expensive than providing salary increases that allow a faculty member to accumulate a comparable sum to cover college costs (Silander 1983). Policy development and cost containment could be complicated when benefits to faculty are shared with other employees of the institution, and decisions for one group of employees could dramatically affect what can be offered—and at what cost—to another group. While cutting back benefits is also an option, it is not usually an easy or popular alternative—especially at institutions where collective bargaining is the norm and where agreement on benefit packages is often a source of strain (Calais 1991). Responsible, careful, and sometimes creative planning, however, can allow for satisfactory benefits without overburdening institutional budgets or forcing unnecessary retrenchment in monetary or quasi-monetary forms of compensation—the challenge for those involved in setting and implementing policy on compensation.

Benefits have grown in importance and cost. Many faculty gain by taking large portions of their compensation in the form of fringe benefits. Fringe benefits assist faculty collectively, if not always individually—including cheaper costs for groups rather than individuals, avoidance of "adverse selection" policies in large group packages, nontaxation of employee-provided benefits, a higher share of benefits overall in union-influenced settings, and better retirement systems through economies of scale (Hamermesh 1988). While some academic employers might try to shift greater shares of the cost of health care and some other reductions to faculty, overall colleges and universities as well as faculty are becoming more knowledgeable consumers of benefit programs.

Key Concepts and Fundamentals of Practices Affecting Benefits

Certain concepts have always been fundamental to the discussion of compensation theory, as evidenced in the large literature on compensation and satisfaction in business, sociology, public administration, and similar fields. These concepts appear to reflect the fundamentals found in many learning and behavior modification theories in education as well. Basically, a recognizable connection should exist between compensation and performance, which is facilitated, and the meaning of the connection enhanced, by tying the timing of the reward closely to the appropriate performance. Next, the level of performance required for the reward needs to be attainable, and the reward system needs to be of value to the persons for whom it is intended. Finally, the compensation process has to be open and understood by those involved.

In addition to these fundamentals, faculty compensation is generally based on the criteria of worth, equity, need, and market influences (Silander 1983). Worth in academic settings is an assessment and rewarding of research, teaching, and service, while equity (or fairness) relates to "compensation based on comparative responsibilities" (p. 22). The criterion of need covers primarily the area of fringe benefits and will likely vary as faculty and their needs change. (Market influences affecting compensation are discussed later.) Finally, compensation policies and structures do, or should, reflect legal requirements, especially those related to women and minorities, and they should be cost-effective and efficient (Silander 1983).

The fundamentals of the process and criteria are important considerations in designing compensation policies. Understanding how compensation is actually structured is important to institutional policy planners and decision makers, as well as to those affected by the policies and practices—namely, the faculty. Many factors contribute to variations in the structure of compensation for faculty today. For instance, figures usually reflect a nine-month period, unlike in the private sector, where compensation is based on a twelve-month calendar. Faculty compensation structures also reflect other aspects of academic organization, such as rank, tenure, and full-time and part-time work load. It is important, therefore, to consider the multiple ways compensation is structured as well as those factors that reflect or influence the process of establishing compensation.

Primary factors affecting the structure of compensation are the type of institution and the institution's mission. A research university might formulate policies that reflect very different values from those of a two-year community college. A public institution differs from a private one. The compensation structure of a "knowledge-work" organization might be very different from that employed in a relatively simple service business or a manufacturing firm, for the skills required of employees in these two kinds of organizations differ significantly (Lawler 1990). Institutions involved in collective bargaining contracts might structure compensation differently from those without bargaining units. Moreover, the structure of compensation can vary as much within an institution as across institutions, especially in large, complex institutions or systems. It might be a function of mission and market interaction and of variations that reflect disciplinary differences.

Compensation as reward
Many of the approaches found in empirical analyses are borne out in the research on compensation to one degree or another. Tuckman's important work on faculty reward structures (1976) reviews several approaches to compensation structure that were at the forefront in shaping policy, including various models of supply and demand posited by Brown (1965) and Freeman (1975). A perspective on compensation based on a human capital framework (Johnson and Stafford 1974) increased awareness of the connection between earnings and experience in the academic marketplace. (Other studies have looked at specific variables that might affect the determination of salary, including work load [Katz 1973], discipline, rank, and experience [Koch and Chizmar 1973], and gender [Ferber 1971].)

Unconvinced that any of the studies he reviewed explained the structure of compensation fully, Tuckman designed his own conceptual model of the academic reward structure, of which compensation per se was a substantial but not sole component (1976, H. Tuckman 1979). His model suggests an interplay between academic product and labor markets on the one hand and institutional reward systems on the other hand. He concludes that economic events affect both faculty salaries and the academic reward structure, which in turn affect the way faculty spend their time. As a result of continual changes in the academic product and labor markets, the availability of academic rewards and their impact on faculty performance is continually in flux. Tuckman's early work and his own and others' research that built on this conceptual model have long influenced the way we have thought about the structure of compensation and faculty reward systems (see, e.g., Mortimer, Bagshaw, and Masland 1985; Tuckman and Tuckman 1980; Tuckman and Pickerill 1988).

Compensation as strategic pay

A more recent and equally significant study suggests that compensation should be aligned with an organization's strategic direction (Lawler 1990). This idea goes beyond the suggestion that institutional mission affects compensation. Strategic pay implies that careful thought be given to the objectives of compensation systems and that these objectives relate closely to an institution's strategic plan and to the behaviors required to achieve that plan. Effective compensation policies, then, are those that support and reinforce the organization's objectives and the kind of culture, climate, and behaviors needed to effectively meet those objectives. While this statement sounds logical, many times neither business nor academe takes this approach to compensation policies and planning (Lawler 1990). Instead, most pay practices tend to produce hierarchical, rigid organizational cultures with low levels of teamwork and cooperation, and they do not tend to motivate organizationally effective behavior. If we reflect on the often inconsistent relationship between institutional mission and what is rewarded, it is clear that this critique of compensation structures applies to many colleges and universities.

The idea of strategic pay involves a series of core principles and considerations that form the basis for structuring compensation (Lawler 1990). Although the idea reflects certain philosophies of the private sector, the underlying framework fits equally well in academic settings, especially in periods of economic restrictions and fluctuations in the market. First, the structure of any institutional reward system should be based on core principles that indicate how an organization intends to operate. In education, we blithely refer to those core principles as "mission statements." According to Lawler's definition, however, we would be only half right. While core principles should reflect basic organizational values similar to those found in academic mission statements, they also need to reflect the institution's operating environment and considerations of affordability (see also Cameron 1984, Chaffee 1985, and Keller 1983). Compensation affects organizational performance and individual behavior because of its impact on individual beliefs and expectations about rewards. These expectations in turn influence motivation and organizational culture, as well as who is attracted to and who is retained by the institution. Therefore, to maximize effectiveness, core principles should stay basically the same unless strategic organizational changes have occurred, allowing for continued connection between core principles and organizational strategy (Lawler 1990).

Several key decision points are also central components in the development of strategic compensation (Lawler 1990). The first has to do with paying for performance. People readily acknowledge that they expect to be paid for work completed and, further, would like to be paid well for work done well. Yet most people in most organizations admit they perceive a gap between desired and actual pay for performance. Thus, effective policies should not only reinforce payment for performance but specify what kind of performance will be rewarded. It could vary by institutional type or discipline, but it should not be left to the individual faculty member to guess. Desired activities should be clarified and consistently reinforced through compensation practices. Further, organizational strategy, activities that are professed to be important, and those that are actually rewarded should be clearly linked.

The second decision point has to do with how base pay is determined (Lawler 1990). In business, the base for pay usually comes from a thorough job assessment, which allows for a certain comparability across like positions. An alternative method for determining base pay comes from an assessment of individual characteristics, including personal skills that the organization values. The latter approach might also be more prevalent in knowledge-based organizations like colleges and universities, where position descriptions per se are not enough to determine base pay across disciplines and rank.

However base pay is determined, the criteria should be clearly identified to avoid confusion and to verify the connection between base pay as a component of overall compensation and the organization's strategic direction.

Market position (how well one is paid when compared to peers in other institutions) is a third decision point in structuring compensation (Lawler 1990). Among faculty of all types of institutions, pay remains a primary reason for leaving an institution (Breneman and Youn 1988; Burke 1987; Gamson, Finnegan, and Youn 1990; Matier 1990). Given an institution's mission and financial resources, it might not be feasible to compete broadly to attract or retain faculty. Nevertheless, policy planners need to have sound principles related to variability in the market and competition for ethical reasons and to manage faculty perceptions, for in many respects, equitable compensation is perceptual.

Among faculty of all types of institutions, pay remains a primary reason for leaving an institution.

The development of sound principles is complicated by the difficulty in defining the internal and external institutional market. Factors like geography, type of institution, institutional mission, discipline, and seniority might all come into play. Some of the ambiguity is mitigated by a focus on organizational structure and strategy, and the determination of internal and/or external equity in compensation. Single-purpose organizations, those concentrating on a primary product or service, often strive toward internal equity reinforced by a constancy of purpose and single culture (Lawler 1990; Leap 1991). For example, a small college with a religious mission and a holistic focus on teaching might decide to reward its faculty solely on rank and years of experience to strengthen institutional homogeneity and weaken disciplinary differences. Conversely, organizations like universities with multiple missions and multiple cultures might find it more strategically important to foster external equity in compensation. The emphasis is on defining the market(s) clearly and striving toward either internal or external equity in compensation for the benefit of faculty and organizational effectiveness.

The final two decision points are the role of benefits and the process of structuring compensation (Lawler 1990). Benefit programs play a role in strategic compensation, and they convey meaning to constituents, in this case to faculty (Lawler 1990). High benefit levels translate into presumed long-term relationships, job stability, and concern for employees, while lower benefit levels reflect priorities like entrepreneurial activity and allow for flexible labor costs. One part of policy planning is to recognize that institutional meaning exists in the development of benefit packages and of the compensation structure in general. Further, planners need to understand the way in which faculty interpret benefits.

A second part of planning policy comes in planning an effective compensation structure. Part of this understanding results from who participates in the design of compensation structures. When institutions rely too heavily on senior administrators or personnel officers to determine compensation structures or if such persons are the only participants in key decision points, little opportunity might be available for compensation to serve its intended purposes within the overall organizational strategy. This review found evidence to support primary reliance on nonfaculty for the development of compensation structures and a lack of congruence between organizational purpose, faculty values, and compensation structures. At some point, if compensation is to have meaning, if it is to foster strategically appropriate behaviors by faculty, and if it is intended to retain quality faculty, compensation must be structured so as to represent both institutional and faculty values. Without input from faculty, it is difficult to see how the latter could be effectively achieved.

Summary
Twenty-five years ago, it might have been possible to establish a fairly monolithic compensation structure that would adequately serve the faculty's needs while reinforcing the institution's priorities. Today's colleges and universities, however, are complex institutions often with multiple missions and very diverse faculty, although many are trying to employ compensation structures that have not changed much since the mid-1960s.

Any effective reappraisal of compensation will involve thinking differently about compensation and its link with faculty morale, fiscal responsibility, and economic restraints. Policy planners and decision makers need to recognize the meaning conveyed by reward systems and compensation structures to faculty and to prospective employees. For example, what is included in quasi-monetary and nonfinancial benefits often communicates an institution's concern for the well-being and quality of life of its faculty and staff. These components of compensation can be especially important when salaries themselves cannot be continually increased or when base salaries might not be as competitive. The ability to offer quality benefits to the faculty at reasonable costs to the institution is becoming more difficult. Personnel officers need to be well versed in the alternatives and the trade-offs in cost of delivery systems like cafeteria-style benefit programs, and be willing to receive regular input from faculty and staff about changing needs.

Because compensation systems convey meaning to employees, it is important that they reflect the strategic direction of the institution rather than mirroring a loosely connected mix of old and new institutional priorities. The structure of compensation should reflect core principles of the institution (its mission) and the value it places on various work constructs. In addition, market position and issues of collective bargaining and retirement programs should be taken into account in structuring compensation.

Finally, who should be involved in developing compensation structures has shifted from a primarily administrative task to one that is more inclusive of those directly affected by the policies—the faculty. To be effective, to induce strategic activities, and to facilitate the recruitment and retention of quality faculty, compensation structures must reflect what is of value both to the institution and to the faculty. Inherent in this statement is the fact that most institutions will no longer be able to construct monolithic compensation systems that will adequately serve their faculty. As a result, more careful analysis and comprehensive planning will be required so that one outmoded system is not replaced by many contradictory and/or discriminating compensation structures. Internal and external market forces are increasingly influential; many institutions are already working with their faculty to develop meaningful compensation structures that provide the quality and kinds of monetary and nonfinancial benefits that are of value and that can be supported in an era of increased economic instability. Understanding the process of developing compensation structures and the meaning ascribed to them is a first step in accomplishing this task.

FACTORS AFFECTING THE STRUCTURE OF COMPENSATION

Among several factors affecting the structure of compensation at colleges and universities, three in particular deserve attention and are addressed in this section, albeit briefly: external and internal labor markets for faculty; collective bargaining, which, when in effect, directly influences compensation structures; and retirement policies and early retirement incentive programs, which deserve special note for their impact on the structure of compensation, especially for a graying professoriat.

The Academic Labor Market

Traditional theories of the labor market have often been based on the principle of supply and demand. If the supply is great and the demand is low, the price of labor goes down; conversely, if the supply is low and the demand is great, the price goes up. In higher education systems, analysts and researchers suggest that private-sector theories might be somewhat simplistic for understanding academic labor markets, that many overlapping markets operate in educational systems, confounding labor pool forecasting and complicating formulas for compensation (Breneman and Youn 1988). Among indices deriving from multiple market factors, higher education policy makers need to consider varying institutional missions that can lead to different priorities for hiring and therefore different labor markets. For example, distinctions are made between research/graduate training and undergraduate teaching. Further, variations in disciplines result from a combination of multiple supply-and-demand factors compounded by technological advances in some fields and increased specialization or segmentation in others (Breneman and Youn 1988; Youn 1988; Youn and Zelterman 1988). The field of biology is a case in point: As the field has fragmented into multiple, highly specialized submarkets, the "price" of faculty can vary considerably, depending on the type of biologist sought.

Institutional policy makers need to consider that many market forecasts have been based on traditional labor market data, compiled from three primary, outdated assumptions related to inflow, outflow, and career paths. Previously, we believed that faculty inflow consisted of those coming directly from graduate school who were, on average, in their early thirties and who would be around for a while in the institution. Faculty outflow was presumed to consist primarily of retirees at traditional retirement age (65). And we have long believed that, while faculty might change institutions throughout their careers, they always stay somewhere within the higher education system, thus making reentry into institutional academic settings a fairly easy adjustment. Today, these assumptions are true at fewer types of institutions and for fewer faculty across institutions. Traditional considerations do not fully account for the change in individual faculty members' perspectives—their view of the profession itself, the institutional climate, perceived opportunities for mobility, preferred work priorities, career perspectives, and so on. The individual perspective becomes even more complicated and more removed from traditional institutional expectations when many prospective faculty candidates are employed outside academe, often having had several career experiences and sometimes involving more than one specialty, such as English and telecommunications, which is more often the circumstance today.

These thoughts provide a mere introduction to the complexities of the academic labor market that serves as a significant determinant of the structure of compensation in higher education.

External Market Issues

Recent federal legislation uncapping retirement has caused renewed discussion about the higher education labor market. Particular attention has been drawn to the age structure of the academic work force, to the prospective pool of replacement candidates, and, indirectly, to how faculty are remunerated. The academic work force by 2000 will see a large reduction, as much as 40 percent, in senior faculty because of retirement, and replacements for these departing scholars are not entirely evident (Schuster 1990).

Supply and demand

How much of a reduction in its academic work force each institution will experience varies considerably. Some optimists predict that the academic labor market in general is apt to rebound in the late 1990s as a result of expanded enrollments from children of the baby boomers and the need to replace retirees (Schuster 1990). Others interpret less favorably the effect of enrollment projections, but they usually do agree on the impending impact of retirements on the academic labor market (National Research Council 1989). If the portrayal of our colleges and universities as inverted pyramids of age and rank (Hacker 1992) can be generalized, many, if

not most, institutions will face significant numbers of retirements through the turn of the century. Studies of four-year
institutions nationally show vacancies as high as 50 percent
in the last half of the decade; the seven-campus Minnesota
system, for example, reports an approximate 70 percent retirement rate for the same time period (Bowen and Sosa 1989;
Schuster 1990). Institutions can look forward, as a conservative
annual average, to a 4 percent attrition rate, which translates
into 1.3 percent retirements and deaths, and 2.7 percent
departures.

On the supply side, the most dramatic shortages will come
between 1997 and 2002, with only four candidates available
for every five academic openings (Gamson, Finnegan, and
Youn 1990). Adding to the dilemma is the fact that most studies look only at full-time and tenured faculty, which means
that part-time and junior faculty are not reflected in predic-
tions about attrition (Bowen and Schuster 1986). Given that
assistant professors account for the bulk of new hires annually
(Burke 1987) and for a substantial portion of those who leave
an institution in any given year, higher education policy
planners and decision makers should pay particular attention
to this group. The total cost involved in hiring, including the
resources spent on faculty who do not succeed in the system,
can be staggering.

Today, the total supply of faculty is hard to describe or measure. Throughout the 1980s, increasingly smaller portions of
the best and brightest students went into academic careers.
The number of doctorates granted to U.S. citizens has been
decreasing (Dooris and Lozier 1989), resulting in an increasingly international faculty pool who might or might not return
to their native countries for employment. Prospective increases
in doctoral recipients as a result of growth in undergraduate
enrollments will not assist in filling faculty vacancies for at
least ten years (National Research Council 1989). At that point,
we are still referring to junior, untenured faculty who must
succeed and stay in the system to truly alleviate academic
shortages. In addition, institutions have not relied primarily
on a pool of part-time faculty as the source of their full-time
staffs. Most disciplines have not been forced to consider the
institutional attractiveness of a pool consisting of those who
were not hired into academe at earlier career stages and/or
who have built careers entirely outside the educational enterprise (Schuster 1990).

Many institutions have been forced to become more creative in generating a prospective faculty pool, for example, delayed or phased retirement plans for faculty in disciplines with current and future shortages (McGuire and Price 1989), stockpiling faculty by conducting searches and filling positions in advance of actual needs for replacement (Gamson, Finnegan, and Youn 1990), and hiring persons without terminal degrees and providing institutional support as they complete their degrees with the intent of hiring the person as a faculty member (Gamson, Finnegan, and Youn 1990). Not only do these alternative pools confound our knowledge of faculty supply, but they also raise issues about training, expertise, expectations, and compensation in the wake of what has already been deemed an imperiled national resource—the professoriat (Bowen and Schuster 1986).

Any discussion of the pool of applicants seems to lead to the idea that quantity is the most important factor in meeting a given need. Certainly, a quantitative shortage of faculty is a significant issue in addressing needs of the academic labor market in the next decade. Yet sufficient numbers of faculty cannot unilaterally ensure the necessary work force. Institutional and disciplinary fit become important criteria that limit a simple numerical resolution to the dilemma of the labor market (see Breneman and Youn 1988 for a discussion of multiple markets). For example, a recent study found that institutions are already having difficulty filling positions in high-demand fields (El-Khawas 1989), and another national study of faculty found "sizable proportions of faculty members indicat[ing] that they would consider leaving their institutions, and higher education altogether," if the right opportunity came along (Schuster 1990, p. 37). By the nature of the work they do, the "right opportunity" might exist more frequently for faculty in some disciplines and in some institutions than in others. An inadequate supply could lead to increased "institution raiding" in certain disciplines and for certain academics, especially minority faculty. If an institution or department has the resources, the rich can get richer *if* faculty can be retained or "stolen"; in less fortunate disciplines and institutions, the outlook is dim if competition increases.

Academic salaries compared to the private sector
When planning to replace retirees and fill other vacancies, in addition to concerns about the pool itself, senior admin-

istrators are often concerned that faculty salaries have declined when compared to salaries in business, industry, and other professions. The subject of a decline in faculty salaries is controversial. Some argue that steady growth has occurred in recent years, that academics are gaining (or have already gained) ground lost in the late 1960s and early 1970s. Others construct the debate as one of confusion between real dollars and relative dollars (Bowen and Schuster 1986; Hansen 1985).

The annual reports on the economic status of the academic profession by the American Association of University Professors (AAUP) suggest that improvement in faculty salaries is

FIGURE 1

ONE-YEAR CHANGES IN FACULTY SALARIES, 1972-73 TO 1992-93

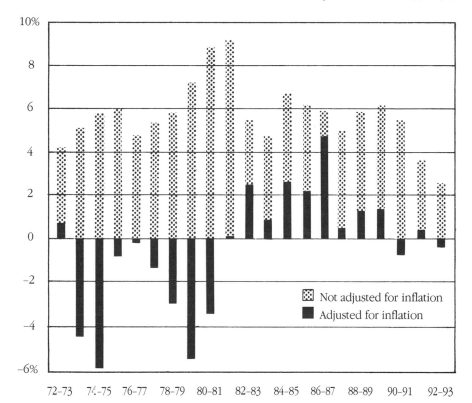

Note: Salaries are adjusted for inflation as measured by the Consumer Price Index for periods from December to December.
Source: AAUP, cited in *Chronicle of Higher Education,* 14 April 1993, p. A19. Reprinted with permission.

more apparent than real when compared to increases in the rate of inflation (see, e.g., Annual Report 1990, 1991). According to Committee Z of the AAUP, which prepares the annual reports, the average salary increases of faculty in the 1980s were smaller than the average annual rate of real dollar losses felt in the 1970s (Annual Report 1990, p. 3) (see figure 1). Many other professions were subject to the same salary declines in the 1970s, yet most have already regained their former levels. For the professoriat, recovery has been much slower.

These fluctuations in salary levels are relevant to a larger discussion of compensation for several reasons. First, as a result of disparity between salary losses, gains, and recovery, long-standing faculty often have far less purchasing power than new colleagues. In 1989–90, average salaries, adjusted for inflation, were still below 1970–71 rates for continuing faculty (Annual Report 1990, p. 3). The salary compression that results from such disparity affects collegiality, morale, perceptions of careers, and campus budgets, especially at those institutions with merit pay systems. A decline in real salaries compared to other professions and the private sector also has implications for an institution's ability to recruit prospective faculty from nonacademic settings. The variance between salaries in academe and the private sector could be substantial for those brought in as assistant professors; the gap might be unbridgeable for associate or full professors. The variance is true not only in highly competitive disciplines, such as computer science, but also in many professional disciplines like public administration and educational administration that draw on markets other than higher education for experienced practitioners. Consideration of the composition of an alternative pool for new faculty might force these economic realities upon institutions in a period when decision makers are least able to accommodate such salary negotiations.

Finally, the disparity in academic and private-sector salaries has an effect on graduate students considering careers in academe. The indebtedness facing students after six or more years of advanced education is far greater today than in earlier times, in part as a result of the shift in student financial aid from grants-in-aid to loans. Potential new faculty members are more likely to be encumbered with debt than the faculty who trained them and who themselves benefited from assistantships, fellowships, or the GI Bill. This debt adds a different dimension to the normal considerations of entry-level salary and to career outlooks. A fundamental question arises as to whether graduate students with significant debt can afford to take assistant professor positions in many fields at many institutions if their salary levels will barely keep pace with inflation.

Traditional and nontraditional members of the academic labor pool are all affected by the financial circumstances of the last 20 years. Reconciling life circumstances, collegiate and noncollegiate competition for professionals, and what appears to be ever-decreasing institutional budgets (in real dollars) create new challenges for institutional policy makers that are not likely to subside in the foreseeable future.

Internal Labor Market Issues
Faculty as independent professionals within a multidisciplinary market
In addition to the overall labor market picture for faculty external to the institution, a number of internal changes in the labor market must be recognized in a comprehensive approach to faculty compensation. One fundamental change has been the growth and expansion of colleges and universities since World War II, which has altered the nature of the profession. Academe is no longer considered a closed collection of scholars who share an overriding vision. Collegiate institutions are more accurately characterized as collectives of disciplines, departments, agendas, and visions. An individual faculty member applies to and is hired into a department and its philosophies, policies, and practices as much as into the larger institution. The departmental orientation of the academic profession renders faculty more subject to the market fluctuations affecting individual disciplines.

In the late 1970s and 1980s, for instance, demand from the private sector for people with training in fields like engineering and computer science expanded quickly and accentuated the need for faculty members and new students in these disciplines (Hansen 1985). It is not uncommon for professors of computer science to be paid nearly half again as much as colleagues in traditional liberal arts fields. Such market influences could be particularly noticeable in research universities and highly selective colleges where hiring and compensation practices might vary considerably among disciplines and departments. Some smaller institutions have tried to maintain

Academe is no longer considered a closed collection of scholars who share an overriding vision.

salary structures that ignore disciplinary markets in favor of rank and years of service, but in larger institutions, particularly for science, engineering, and business, market differentiation is a strong factor.

The multidisciplinary orientation of large parts of academe compels faculty members to become more sophisticated players in the marketplace. By accepting and fostering the symbols of status and prestige associated with particular disciplines, including the related monetary awards, faculty perpetuate the market-driven differentiation and competition between and among disciplines and institutions. A multidisciplinary orientation to the professoriat also means that analysis of supply and demand becomes a more intricate task for institutional policy planners and decision makers (see, e.g., Bowen and Sosa 1989; El-Khawas 1989; and Gamson, Finnegan, and Youn 1990 for discussions of the effects of discipline on the faculty labor market and differences associated with institutional type). Suffice it to say that faculty members entering or maneuvering in the marketplace today need to be rather sophisticated players in what can be a highly complex and differentiated compensation game.

Collective bargaining as an alternative to multidisciplinary markets

When collective bargaining first burst onto the collegiate scene in the early 1970s, it was argued that bargaining agreements would enhance salary levels and other aspects of faculty life. After two decades, the research is inconclusive as to whether collective bargaining has advanced the salaries of unionized faculty far and above those of their nonunionized colleagues. Studies have shown that effects of collective bargaining on salaries and compensation have varied over time and across institutional type, and that the real impact might have been felt more in governance than in compensation (Baker 1984; Barbezat 1987a). The portion of the total American labor force that is unionized was about 30 percent in the early 1960s and only 16 percent by the late 1980s. Unionization on campus has been stagnant since the early 1980s (Hamermesh and Woodbury 1991).

Faculty who organized early in the 1970s tended to reap significant initial benefits from unionization, but that early advantage in salaries has declined considerably (Becker 1985). Those who organized more recently probably gained a smaller initial margin of advantage over nonunion colleagues. The impact of collective bargaining on improving compensation seems to be initially significant but with waning long-term effects. This trend could be a reflection of the emphasis placed on economic issues in the early years of a contract when it is important in winning faculty members' support for highly visible gains to be apparent (Baker 1984). Another explanation could be that the removal of merit pay and other rewards based on individual differences from unionized compensation programs could cause salaries to rise more slowly (Leap 1991). To understand the true impact of collective bargaining on faculty life, we should look at indirect effects of the presence of unions on a campus, even if the faculty are not unionized, and the effect of being in more heavily unionized states than others (Hamermesh and Woodbury 1991).

Across institutional types, unionization seems to have had a greater overall effect on salaries at two-year colleges and at small, private four-year colleges (Barbezat 1987a; Becker 1985). Faculty at major universities appear to have received fewer immediate or long-term compensation benefits from organizing—which could be in part a function of the comparatively higher salaries of faculty in such institutions.

For colleges and universities themselves, collective bargaining has provided a degree of stabilization in policies and practices affecting faculty, particularly in making compensation policies routine and centralized. Fairness, equality, and justice in compensation practices are defined as part of the negotiation process, and formal procedures are prescribed and followed closely (Becker 1985; Milkovich and Newman 1990). Such procedures address pay rates, types of pay to be received, and the way decisions about compensation will be made and administered. While important benefits are derived from the standardization of institutional practices that occur as a result of unionization, costs are incurred as well. In terms of issues affecting compensation, once a contract is signed, the institution is locked into the conditions of the contract for its duration, and some fear it could prohibit the college or university from adequately responding to fluctuating market conditions or to the changing needs of faculty.

Although collective bargaining agreements have delivered on many of their original promises, their use in addressing current complex issues of compensation remains to be seen. Standard union policies might need to change to offer the range of alternatives required to adequately address compensation needs of new faculty. It remains unclear why collective bargaining gains do not continue, but in the years ahead, we will have opportunities to observe the effectiveness of collective bargaining negotiators in maintaining adequate salaries and benefits in periods of declining resources.

New contractual arrangements

Other differences in the nature of the internal academic labor market affect compensation policies and practices. Already briefly mentioned are differences resulting from a changing external pool of candidates, variation in and range of competitive salaries within and between academic organizations, and alterations resulting from a change in nature of the academic profession itself. In addition, or perhaps as a result of some of these changes, variations have become more frequent in the structure of academic careers and positions themselves. For instance, traditional tenure positions at many institutions are becoming less numerous as institutions mature and prepare to respond to changing environmental forces. Variation also occurs, in part, because of an aging faculty, an oversupply of faculty in some fields, and an undersupply in others (Leslie 1989). Clinical appointments, as departures from full-time tenure-track professorships, have been common in medical fields for years, but more recently, the number of clinical appointments in nonmedical fields like education has increased. Whether the reference is to positions as instructors, graduate teaching assistantships, term contracts, or suspension of the up-and-out policy to afford longer relationships with an institution, academic staffing patterns are becoming more varied at all kinds of four-year colleges and universities (Braudy 1988; Miller 1987).

Just over one-third of all faculty nationally are in part-time positions, although certainly this percentage varies by institutional type, with labels like temporary, visiting, courtesy, joint, and interdisciplinary. Often these appointments are a result of noncontinuous funding sources, term appointments, or specified assignments. More recent approaches include two persons sharing one appointment (sometimes, but not always, a strategy to accommodate dual-career couples) and phased retirement programs that allow faculty to receive retirement benefits earlier in exchange for a reduced teaching assignment (Leslie 1989). Faculty and administrators have

become very creative in developing myriad new kinds of contractual or compensatory arrangements, such as collaborative
pay arrangements or consulting contracts. At the same time,
these creative relationships raise a variety of management and
ethical issues an institution must face, including hidden costs
of monitoring and socializing nontraditional staff, and threats
of exploitation (Flynn et al. 1986; Gappa 1984; Leslie 1989;
Waggamon 1983). In short, the variety of departures from the
traditional model for faculty careers—full-time, one institution—is a trend that must be addressed within any discussion
of compensation (see Gappa and Leslie 1993 for a full discussion of the issues associated with nontraditional staffing).

Retirement and its relationship to compensation
New legislation regarding mandatory retirement and the trend
for faculty to remain in the work force to an older age are
creating a new area of concern for policy makers dealing with
compensation and personnel. Numerous issues are related
to policies and practices affecting retirement, and they are
only beginning to be considered in light of the changing academic environment. Concerns include the "appropriate"
retirement age, the cost of early retirement incentives, benefit
packages for retirees who are living longer and want to remain
active in their academic communities, and the effects of a
large pool of senior faculty with an extended time to retirement on the ability of an institution to recruit, retain, and
appropriately compensate more junior faculty or for that
senior pool to supplant other faculty retirements in lieu of
new hires. Policy planners must be aware of institutional
trade-offs, the potential effects on the curriculum and delivery
of academic programs, career implications for junior and
senior faculty, salary compression, and unintentional effects
of initial solutions.

In a holistic look at faculty compensation, policies and practices affecting retirement must be considered to develop
appropriate institutional responses to present and future
needs. One reason for this focus is that two of the largest
fringe benefits (retirement and social security) remain with
the employee in some proportion throughout his or her institutional career and into retirement (Annual Report 1990). Policy planners have been forced to reconsider the long-term
impact of fringe benefits and salary distributions on the institution's financial health as a result of this continuing financial

relationship and because of additional pressure from external economic and legislative changes, such as modifications in tax laws and the uncapping of the retirement ceiling (see, e.g., Anderson and Meyerson 1987; Calais 1991). The economic impact of 20 to 30 or more years of retirement or pension and modified benefit payments to faculty in an era of continually escalating costs can be staggering. Such a financial commitment also affects an institution's ability to offer competitive salary and benefit packages to its present employees and to the faculty it hopes to recruit. This perspective could challenge assumptions about early retirement programs and their ability to free institutional resources. If nothing else, realization of the long-term effects of salary and benefit packages should alter the equations used in economic forecasting and the development of compensation policy.

Early retirement incentives and programs

Changes in tax laws limit the financial inducements institutions can use to design early retirement plans (Lee 1989). Early retirement incentive programs always raise a concern about who will be encouraged to participate—the most productive or the least productive people? An important consideration in developing such programs is to identify which areas within the institution are likely to experience future shortages in work load, so that appropriate decisions about recruitment and early retirement are possible. One study of research universities, for instance, shows serious shortages expected in arts and sciences faculty in the 1990s, in part because of retirements and a decline in the number of persons pursuing faculty careers in these disciplines (Lozier and Dooris 1987). Faculty in business, computer science, allied health, and law tend to be younger, so they are potentially able to stay longer with an institution (Lozier and Dooris 1987). At the same time, faculty in these fields are more likely to exit academe altogether, being offered more lucrative employment opportunities in the private sector. To account for and adjust to the variations across disciplines requires more vigorous and ongoing forecasting about institutions and the labor market than might have been necessary in the past. Forecasting allows decision makers to gather data on numbers of faculty and to project compensation costs for those likely to retire and those likely to stay in the system.

In addition to institutional forecasting based on numeric data, policy planners must understand what motivates faculty to leave an institution and/or to take early retirement. This critical piece is often missing in the design of personnel policies, including early retirement plans. For instance, one study of faculty at a research university found a direct link between compensation policies and participation in early retirement programs. The type and number of benefits offered in early retirement plans were the most important factors mentioned for participation (Kellams and Chronister 1987). A national study of faculty and retirement found that two of the top three factors affecting the decision to retire were related to compensation: overall financial status and eligibility for full retirement benefits (Lozier and Dooris, cited in Schoenfeld 1992). The availability of early retirement benefits was of only marginal importance, however.

Other factors determining participation in early retirement plans are professional problems (e.g., burnout), institutional problems, and attractive alternatives within the university or in other universities (Amey 1991; Kellams and Chronister 1987). These factors at first glance seem less related to compensation, although what constitutes an attractive alternative could be connected to monetary or nonfinancial compensation. Changes in work load, clientele, work schedule, and opportunities to collaborate with others, for example, are elements of offers that might be quite appealing to older faculty. Of considerable consequence in decisions to retire is also the desire for more personal and family time, again, a factor apart from traditional compensation policies (Lozier and Dooris, cited in Schoenfeld 1992). Most important, such studies show that productive faculty are as likely to take early retirement as unproductive faculty—but for different reasons. Understanding these variables is important to successful planning and directly affects strategic structuring of compensation.

Early retirement incentive programs take one of two forms, and each has a different long-term effect on the structure and costs of institutional compensation. The first kind includes *formal programs,* with specific criteria applied to all faculty in a selected class. The second, and more flexible, kind includes *ad hoc programs* that provide for negotiation of incentives with each individual faculty member. Ad hoc programs might include severance pay or lump-sum payments, annuity enhancements, liberalized actuarial reduction, bridge benefits, and phased or partial retirement (Chronister 1990). Given institutional profiles, one or the other or both programs might be appropriate to provide a complement of options to faculty. For this discussion, the important elements for consideration are that different approaches to early retirement incentive programs exist and that several factors are necessary to determine which program will be cost-effective and attractive to faculty in a given college or university. Those in the forefront in personnel and compensation planning and research suggest that the only way to develop farsighted retirement policies is to be willing to address planning comprehensively, for changes in policies and practices in one area can significantly affect those in another.

Summary
Most institutional practices affecting hiring and compensation were developed in an earlier time under different, more stable conditions. Policy planners need to recognize market changes to develop or modify existing practices of compensation. The traditional market factors of supply and demand have become significant factors in the academic labor market. An overabundance of doctoral degree holders no longer exists in many fields, forcing institutions to compete with the more affluent private sector for scholars and to a greater degree with each other. It is more common today for vacancies to be left open for six months or more, saving money for salaries for the academic unit, at least in the short run. When a vacancy occurs, however, the replacement is not automatically given to the department with the opening. Moreover, vacancies are often filled with persons in lower ranks rather than the one-to-one replacement practices of the past, affecting faculty work load and productivity within the unit (Amey 1992; Burke 1987). Faculty career paths, including intra-academic movement, are more varied today. The list of changes in the internal and external markets goes on and on, often without comparable adjustments in institutional policies and practices regarding compensation.

The complexity of some institutions and the quasi-autonomy of many departments and colleges make one compensation system difficult to achieve and controversial to maintain, except under collective bargaining. To accurately plan effective strategies to address the labor market, institutions must take a new look at factors affecting faculty recruitment and retention, especially those aspects over which the institution has direct control—compensation, promotion, and tenure. The multifaceted nature of attrition and retention as affected by rank, gender, discipline, and career stage—and of the direct effect of compensation—must be recognized. Very few institutions will be immune from these issues in the 1990s. The question then becomes how effective colleges and universities want to be as strategists.

THE USES OF COMPENSATION

Institutional quality is inextricably bound to the quality of the faculty, yet hiring and retaining high-quality faculty members are likely to become increasingly difficult in the years ahead. Therefore, every decision about hiring, tenure, and promotion is important far beyond the monetary considerations involved. Factored into these decisions, in addition to salary and benefits, are other costs for the institution— office and clerical support, laboratory space and equipment, sabbatical leaves, travel, and more. Incentives for productivity and service and compensatory time or money for extra teaching or administrative assignments and other duties also must be included in decisions about compensation. What variables contribute to the structure of compensation should be guided by the relationship of compensation to institutional strategy, as noted earlier. Along with this link to strategy, personnel planners and policy makers need to determine how compensation will be used within the institution. Compensation can be used in multiple ways across academic institutions, perhaps even within a given collegiate setting. It is important to recognize these uses and the meanings faculty give them. A reasonable balance should exist between the professional needs of faculty and the needs of the institution to fulfill its mission and objectives. Compensation serves as a complex bridge between the two.

A reasonable balance should exist between the professional needs of faculty and the needs of the institution to fulfill its mission and objectives.

Compensation as Motivator

One of the more commonly held beliefs about compensation is that it can be used to motivate individuals. If employees are rewarded for specific behavior, they are likely to increase, or at least continue, the behavior. If the reward is withheld, the behavior is likely to decrease or be extinguished. The anticipation of bonuses, increases, promotions, or special compensation is supposed to motivate people to work harder, do more, and achieve their fullest potential. These premises are reinforced by much of the research in business or could be inferred from this research. Systems of reward (compensation) are a powerful determinant of skill, perhaps one of the most powerful, that employees in any organization will develop. The underlying message is that employees will learn what is required to be rewarded if they value the reward system. Thus, the central question becomes whether compensation serves as a motivator for faculty. Given that so many faculty are dissatisfied with their compensation or do not feel they are adequately compensated for their work, perhaps the question should be rephrased: *Can* compensation serve as a motivator for faculty?

Some argue that collegiate faculty are unlike other professionals in today's materialistic society who measure occupational success solely in terms of dollars. They suggest that to assume money is the primary motivator for faculty is to disregard the personal, higher degree of intrinsic and private incentives characteristic of the academic profession (Bellah et al. 1985; H. Tuckman 1979; Woloshin 1986). And they suggest that most professors still hold fast to a different value structure in which academic work is seen as a noble activity, an "absorbing errand" (Clark 1988). On the other hand, one study found that level of compensation was the third most important determinant of faculty morale across institutional type (Bowen and Schuster 1986), as "few conditions will inspire faculty more" than an increase in institutional wealth, especially if it in some way trickles down to faculty salaries (p. 141). Others have noted the relationship between what is rewarded and faculty members' activity (see, e.g., Folger 1984; Hoenack et al. 1986; Levin 1991). Although some faculty at colleges where morale is high said, in one study, that salary levels can have a positive impact on morale, far more faculty at colleges where morale is both high and low indicated that salary levels can have a negative impact on morale (Austin 1987). In other words, while salary levels might not have a positive effect on morale, they are quite likely to have a negative effect. Money might not cause motivation, but a high correlation certainly exists. This concept becomes even more important in an era of negligible annual raises and growing fiscal constraints.

To be sure, many nonmonetary and nonmaterialistic benefits can both motivate and satisfy faculty (O'Briant 1991; Woloshin 1986). They can vary by field, by institutional type (as a result of expectations, culture, and so on), or by career stage (Baldwin and Blackburn 1981; H. Tuckman 1979). Working conditions, flexibility, availability of a stimulating intellectual community, the opportunity and facilities for creating new knowledge, the community's recognition of the importance of academic work, and a sense of pride and belonging are aspects of faculty life many value highly. Yet it is difficult to ascribe dollar values to such aspects, so they can be neglected when developing appropriate compensation packages.

Including nonmonetary benefits in the equation for compensation should not imply that faculty have no interest in the monetary and quasi-monetary components of compensation or for being rewarded appropriately and adequately for their work. But scholars question the effectiveness of using only monetary incentives to increase faculty members' productivity or their desire to stay at an institution (Lawrence 1985; McKeachie 1979). When addressing compensation policies and practices, decision makers need to attend to the full array of conditions that help and hinder faculty performance (Clark 1988). Declining pools for annual raises and rising fiscal challenges will force a more comprehensive approach to compensation as decision makers look for alternate methods of supporting and rewarding faculty members' activity. In the end, policy makers will need to look at compensation holistically and realize the full nature of the professorial role and value structure to develop effective structures for compensation.

Rewarding Productivity

A second prevalent assumption is that institutions use compensation to reward productivity. Economic models based on human capital theory (e.g., Baker, Jensen, and Murphy 1988) and psychosociological models (e.g., Horan 1978; Katz and Kahn 1978) emphasize the link between productivity and rewards. From this perspective, compensation should be structured so that a worker's expected compensation increases with a comparable increase in productivity (Konrad and Pfeffer 1990). Experts on compensation suggest that institutional decision makers should address three basic questions in implementing pay for performance:

1. Is money important to individuals?
2. Should pay increases be based on performance?
3. Are pay increases based on performance?

Although his research did not focus solely on monetary rewards, Tuckman concluded that is was quite reasonable to assume that an institution's reward structure plays an important role in determining how faculty spend their time (H. Tuckman 1979). For example, education deans in one study reportedly felt institutional rewards were very effective in affecting faculty members' behavior, a perspective department heads did not share as optimistically (Milkovich and

Newman 1990). Other researchers have questioned such a direct link between productivity and rewards, based on findings in studies of gender and ethnicity that suggest those in the dominant culture or gender earn more for the same level of productivity (see, e.g., Barbezat 1987b, 1988; Buchele and Aldrich 1985; Dickens and Lang 1985; McElrath 1992). Some evidence also suggests that pay is not often strongly related to performance (Bishop 1987; Lawler 1990; Zenger 1992), that one does not necessarily get a significant pay raise for being significantly more productive. In addition, a long-standing belief remains that nonmonetary rewards are as important in improving the productivity of faculty as monetary compensation (Clark 1988; Woloshin 1986). Working conditions, institutional affiliation, and intellectual climate are just a few nonmonetary considerations that often fall outside the scope of formal institutional reward structures but many faculty find highly important. To understand the link between productivity and compensation, it is helpful to look more closely at two possible connections: merit pay as a vehicle for rewarding (and/or encouraging) productivity, and components of faculty activity (measures of productivity) for which compensation is given.

One approach to rewarding productivity coming under closer scrutiny is the concept of merit pay. Borrowed from business and industry, merit pay refers to the practice of granting annual salary increases intended to reflect the quality of individuals' performance (Hansen 1988b). The popularity of merit pay systems comes from the belief that pay can motivate job performance and, as a result, increase organizational effectiveness (Lawler 1990). An expected benefit of merit pay is that highly able faculty will migrate to performance-based pay systems, such as those with merit pay, while less able faculty will migrate to institutions with non-performance-based pay systems (Zenger 1992). In collegiate settings, one might assume that merit pay would encourage faculty to increase their work on teaching, research, and service, according to the institution's values, thereby strengthening the institution and enhancing its benefits to society and students (Hansen 1988a). Whether merit pay systems produce institutionally valuable outcomes or not, the trend in college and university settings is in the direction of greater use of merit pay in adjusting salary (Camp, Gibbs, and Masters 1988).

Any effective pay-for-performance system, including merit pay, has several components (Silander 1983). It should provide clearly understood criteria for measuring output and establish standards of performance, both of which should be in line with the institution's objectives and mission (Lawler 1990). Herein lie the difficulties with the use of systems like merit pay in higher education. First, to be effective, outcomes and established performance standards must be identified, yet in knowledge-based institutions like colleges and universities, it is often quite difficult to specify the desired product (Lawler 1990). For instance, what is an appropriate performance standard for teaching for an undergraduate teacher that can be established in advance to allow for the implementation of an effective merit system? A percentage of students receiving a certain grade? A specified rating based on students' evaluations? Should the measures vary depending on whether the course is required, a new offering, an upper-division seminar, or a large introductory lecture? Unlike a widget factory, some educational results can resist the level of specificity required in a true merit pay system, which can result in a greater reliance on more quantifiable products, such as "produce an average of two articles a year in refereed journals," but ignores arguably equally important matters like quality or impact.

The second difficulty with using merit pay in higher education is that to support the institution's priorities and mission, mechanisms must be available for moderating the effects of internal and external labor markets. If such mechanisms do not exist, all institutions will end up using the same criteria and rewarding the same activity despite the institution's mission.

Whether the emphasis is on merit pay systems or on other adaptations of pay for performance, a central question in higher education is how various activities can and should be evaluated objectively. In merit pay systems, perceived objectivity in assessment is central to maintaining the tie between pay and performance. If measures perceived to be subjective are used as the bases for decisions, faculty suspect the entire process. In such cases, it is likely that the merit system will not foster the belief that pay is based on performance, nor will it likely influence desirable activity.

On the other hand, in adhering to strictly objective measures, components can often become weighted based on the ease and consistency with which they can be assessed and quantified rather than on how well they reflect quality, the institution's mission or priority, or faculty members' activity. For instance, studies on merit pay have found that research is the component easiest to measure uniformly, primarily through publication records (Hansen 1986, 1988b); therefore, research, or at least publication, carries substantial weight in merit pay systems regardless of the type of institution (Fairweather 1992; Hansen 1988a; H. Tuckman 1979). Teaching portfolios have only begun to offer a more "objective" approach to the evaluation of teaching (Seldin 1990), yet the time involved in preparing and reviewing a portfolio on an annual basis, such as would be required for merit pay evaluations, often causes faculty to shy away from its use. Even at institutions where service is highly valued, the debate continues as to how quality (as opposed to quantity) of service is determined.

Criteria for merit pay will and should vary across institutions to reflect an institution's mission and priorities (Hansen 1988a; Lawler 1990; Silander 1983). The challenge is to develop a system that elicits the desired performance while responding to activity in the labor market. Internally, this challenge means developing a merit pay system that accommodates differences in disciplines while fostering overall institutional mission without encouraging inappropriate inter-institutional comparisons of salaries. Policy makers are faced with the even more difficult challenge of maintaining internal priorities while remaining competitive in the external labor market. In large universities where colleges and departments are semiautonomous entities, it is often extremely difficult to implement a consistent and coherent merit system across all units.

In addition to the problem of developing an acceptable system of evaluation that is responsive to the market, at issue still is whether merit pay systems actually motivate faculty to improve productivity. Advocates posit that merit pay systems can offer economic rewards sufficient to attract, develop, and retain faculty who effectively do their job and that they should be the objectives of any compensation practice geared toward increasing productivity (Hansen 1988a). Most faculty members have been socialized to believe that merit deserves recognition and reward even if it is not pay per se. Thus, the symbolic value of merit pay might exceed its actual dollar amount.

Critics argue that, at its best, merit pay offers only a rough approximation of an individual's overall performance. Because merit payments usually become part of base salary, the pay system creates an annuity in which the longer the faculty member stays, the more benefits he or she gains from past effective performance. Instead of high salaries that reflect continuous meritorious performance, they might be more indicative of institutional longevity or early (as opposed to steady or later) productivity (Hacker 1992; Lawler 1990; Mott and Mjosland 1989). As a result, total compensation is almost always unrelated to performance at any given time in a merit pay system (Lawler 1990). Furthermore, in general, only a small percentage of employees are rated in the highest performance categories to receive even noticeably greater salary increases than their colleagues, while as high as 80 percent of employees' annual increases cluster within 2 percent of the mean increase (Zenger 1992, p. 199). Then, how well do merit increases reflect quality and performance? And does such a practice encourage productivity for more than a mere handful of faculty?

Institutions using merit pay as a means for improving performance or productivity also need to recognize the implications and effects of such a practice for those employees whose performance is neither extremely good nor extremely bad. Pay-for-performance policies of compensation can be effective in attracting and retaining high performers and in causing low performers to leave the institution. Just as likely, however, such a system will have unintended effects for those in the middle because of the minimal distinctions in annual salary increases between above-average and below-average performers. The result could be that below-average performers are overrewarded and will stay in the institution, while above-average performers are underrewarded and will leave for other places where they receive better compensation (Ehrenberg, Kasper, and Rees 1991; Lawler 1990; Zenger 1992).

Other threats to the integrity of a merit pay system include the perception that pay is really not contingent on performance (Milkovich and Newman 1990), which is often fed by a policy of secrecy about salaries and raises. Bias in ratings could be another problem. For example, one type of publication might be perceived as overrated, positively or negatively. It also sometimes happens that merit rewards are not viewed as rewards, because some faculty members have so inflated their own self-assessments of performance that the raise they receive is viewed as inadequate. Moreover, the administrators of merit pay, department heads and deans, can become concerned with faculty members' satisfaction with pay rather than with job performance. Angry colleagues who receive lower merit raises can consume large amounts of administrators' time and energy, thereby encouraging the weakening of performance standards. Trust and openness are invaluable in operating a merit system but can be eroded by any and all participants.

Few facts about and research on the use of merit pay systems in higher education are available (e.g., several articles in the November/December 1988 issue of *Academe;* research by Hansen 1988), although the debate continues to escalate. While we know that merit pay might not be effective or useful at every type of institution, few generalizable alternatives are posed. Its applicability in unionized institutions, for instance, has varied over time. Merit pay also seems to be on the rise at more heavily graduate- and research-oriented institutions— perhaps because of the relative ease in measuring research and scholarship—although even that practice is being questioned (see Boyer 1990). In any case, more studies are needed on how merit pay systems operate, their effectiveness in rewarding meritorious faculty, the responses of faculty to merit increases, and the relationship, if any, between merit pay systems and post-tenure review. As it is, most organizations claim to have a merit pay system that effectively links pay increases to desired performance, but, in fact, the majority of merit pay systems fail in their objectives to create a perceived relationship between pay and productivity and to reward better performers (Lawler 1990). Part of the dilemma comes from the definition used. A narrow definition of merit pay, for example, focuses on the recognition of individual differences, while a broader perspective views merit pay as a critically important component of an institution's scheme of compensation whose purpose is to improve the quality of its outputs (Hansen 1988a, 1988b). This broader view of merit pay sounds similar to Lawler's idea of strategic pay. If seen in this light, it is necessary to move beyond the statistics of merit pay as a mechanism for increasing salary and look more specifically at the policy issues concerning the use of a pay-for-performance component in faculty compensation for their impact on organizational strategy.

There is no question that considerations of productivity are central not only to campus compensation systems, but also to other aspects of academic life (Creswell 1985). Long exposure to finely graded systems of evaluation and their attendant prestige encourages academics to focus on what and who is considered meritorious. Strong traditions of peer review pervade determinations of scholarly esteem in all fields. Yet it is often the case that criteria and procedures for promotion and tenure are formalized and disseminated but that policies and procedures for awarding salary increases based on performance are not. Instead, such procedures might vary from department to department and from year to year (Hendrickson and Lee 1983). Hence, whether or not a campus administration creates a formal system of merit pay, a strong *informal* merit-based ethos usually exists. Faculty often know—or believe they know—who the best teachers, the most productive researchers, and the most conscientious student advisers and service providers are. The creation of a formal, merit-based system often forces these informal systems into the open, where particular biases or misperceptions can be discovered and where clear, consensus-based values can be articulated. While administration of such a peer-based system still might vary in consistency and integrity, it has value in the act of publicly stating what type and amount of work are valued and communicating that statement widely.

In addition to professional- and campus-based consensus on rewards and incentives for performance, every faculty member has a "psychological contract" (Schein 1980) that guides that individual's understandings and expectations about the amount of work, the rights and privileges that exist and for whom, and the obligations present. But these personal work rules will coincide with departmental or institutional ones only if they can be discussed. Openness about pay for performance is indispensable.

Rewarding Teaching and Research

In the last several years, national attention has focused on the imbalance that exists in the institutional emphases on teaching and research. The issue has been hotly debated in multiple forums, including national meetings of such organizations as the American Association of Higher Education and the American Educational Research Association. Authors and critics have scrambled to get their ideas on the subject into print, ranging from data-based books and journal articles to thought-provoking essays and op ed pieces (see, e.g., Boyer 1990; Cross 1986; Fairweather 1992; Ikenberry 1992; Sacken 1990). Although this monograph does not intend to engage in the debate to the same extent, the issue of how and to what degree an institution rewards each component of faculty activity is germane to a discussion of compensation. It is also central to the issue of pay for performance.

As noted, those components of faculty activity for which objective, agreed-upon measures exist tend to be those that are weighted more heavily in merit pay decisions. That skewed weighting might be reflected in the finding that only productivity in research was positively related to salary (Konrad and Pfeffer 1990). Despite serious rhetoric from administrators and faculty leaders at all institutions to improve the quality of undergraduate teaching and to refocus efforts toward teaching, studies have shown that almost an inverse relationship exists between quality teaching and institutional reward structures (Backhus 1992; Bowen and Schuster 1986; Dillon and Linnell 1980; Fairweather 1992; Konrad and Pfeffer 1990; Marchant and Newman 1991). An exception to the trend has occurred in some very market-driven fields like business or engineering, yet even in those disciplines it is not clear whether higher salaries actually reflect higher-quality teaching or greater productivity or simply competitive demand for trained people (see Gomez-Mejia and Balkin 1992.)

Less obvious until recently is the trend toward positively rewarding objectively assessed activity (read "publications") and negatively rewarding teaching in general. Evidence is now surfacing that this trend exists to a greater degree than ever before across all types of institutions, regardless of mission, with the possible exception of two-year colleges (Backhus 1992; Boyer 1990; Fairweather 1992; Gray, Froh, and Diamond 1991). Regardless of type of four-year institution, for all tenure-track, full-time faculty, "the more time spent on teaching and instruction, the lower the basic salary" (Fairweather 1992, p. 21). Conversely, again across type, "the greater the time spent on research, the higher the compensation" (p. 25) and the greater the number of publications, the greater the level of compensation.

The specific findings of this study (Fairweather 1992) related to differential compensation are particularly interesting, in part because the data are nationally representative, cutting across institutional type and discipline. Many of the results might have been anticipated, but the degree of consistency in compensation for specific activity is more pronounced across institutional type than most administrators and policy makers believe. As expected, faculty who are paid the most at research universities are those who work with graduate students, spend more time on research than teaching, and publish books and articles. The profile of highly paid faculty at doctorate-granting institutions is the same, with the addition of administrative responsibilities to highly rewarded activities. Faculty at comprehensive colleges and universities who are the most highly compensated follow suit, and, most surprising, so do faculty at liberal arts colleges—those institutions long recognized for their commitment to undergraduate teaching. Colleges whose missions have always been primarily quality teaching appear to reward publication as strongly as do research universities. Even when analyzed by rank across type of institution, these findings suggest a negative relationship between undergraduate teaching and compensation. In research, doctorate-granting, comprehensive, and liberal arts colleges and universities, full professors and assistant professors are rewarded for publishing and for spending more time on research than teaching. Only among associate professors are glimmers of balance between work load and compensation present. For faculty at research, doctorate-granting, and comprehensive universities, research, administration, and teaching are all part of the compensation structure for associate professors. At liberal arts colleges, however, teaching remains a negative factor in compensation for associate professors. While not new in direction from earlier reports, the strength and depth of these findings are.

Faculty are generally rewarded at higher levels for research-related activities, administration, and, occasionally, service rather than for teaching. Such practices encourage faculty to pursue nonteaching activities in ever-increasing amounts, including those found outside the institution. The dominance of research universities and the resulting differential policies for rewarding productivity have led many critics to question whether such policies provide a desirable academic environment (Bowen and Schuster 1986; Boyer 1990; Cross 1986). For example, some faculty might prefer to put their energies into teaching but find they must do what is most financially rewarding. Others very invested in research activities that

Even when analyzed by rank across type of institution, these findings suggest a negative relationship between undergraduate teaching and compensation.

inform practice are wary of engaging in them because they might not lead directly or inevitably to publications. Policy planners and senior decision makers might try to revitalize and refocus faculty members' energies toward undergraduate teaching but meet with great resistance because their efforts are not coupled with an adjustment in institutional reward structures. It is as though the compensation structure holds both faculty and administrators captive, unable to establish new balance and priorities. The irony is that in most studies, faculty and administrators at all kinds of colleges and universities agree that a balance should be struck between an emphasis on research and teaching that allows for multiple missions and varying work loads (e.g., Bassis and Guskin 1986; Boyer 1990; Carnegie Foundation 1990; Gray, Froh, and Diamond 1991), but it will be achieved only if institutional compensation structures support and reward the balance—the concept of strategic compensation (Lawler 1990).

Rewarding Rank and Seniority
Another use of compensation in academe has been to reward people based on rank, time in rank, and/or length of service. Faculty rank provides a major source of structure and definition for compensation policies at many, if not most, institutions. Theoretically, assistant professors receive lower levels of compensation than associates who, in turn, receive less than full professors. At those institutions without ranks, usually community and junior colleges, a variation of the customary ranks of instructor, assistant, associate, and full professor is used. Overall, the structure of salaries by rank has remained fairly consistent over the past 15 years (Hansen 1986). This stability could be a result of pay raises distributed equally across all ranks (U.S. Dept. of Education 1987), notwithstanding merit-based systems used on many campuses.

Ranks vary within institutional type and control, however (Annual Report 1991; U.S. Dept. of Education 1987). For instance, reports have found a widening gap between salaries at public and private universities in recent years across all ranks, with the greatest variation found for professors and instructors. The differences are reversed at other types of four-year institutions, where higher salaries are found at public rather than at private institutions. At public, two-year institutions, not only are average salaries in all ranks higher than at private schools, but the gap is increasing.

Perhaps the most interesting variations can be found in rank across academic disciplines. A key trend is the higher salaries of new assistant professors in certain fields (Annual Report 1991; Hansen 1986). Over the seven-year period from 1976–77 to 1983–84, reported salary dispersions for full professors ranged from 45 to 71.2 percent across fields, while the range for new assistant professors was from 25.7 to 84.3 percent (Hansen 1986, p. 106). In most cases, fields with the greatest percentage of salary increases for full professors also saw the most significant increases for new assistant professors, although not necessarily the same percentage. Many of the disciplines that flourished during this period, such as business and engineering, saw greater increases for new assistant professors than for continuing full professors, even though full professors also saw significant increases. Annual salary reports in *Academe* reinforce this trend today.

Evidence also appears in the AAUP's salary reports that new assistant professors in many fields traditionally considered low pay, such as foreign languages, are receiving significantly greater percentage increases in their salaries when compared to full professors and to continuing assistant professors. The variance not only reflects the strong competition between the public and private sectors and across institutions to be able to hire the brightest and best new doctoral recipients, but also could be a result of limited pools of prospective faculty in certain disciplines where demand has been curtailed in the past. Salary dispersion has increased over the last 15 years to the point that some institutions might not be able to afford the going rate for new assistant professors in certain highly demanded fields. As a result of the increasing base salary of entering assistant professors, negative slope and salary compression at all types of institutions are serious threats (Annual Report 1988, 1991). Neither of these situations is easy to ameliorate, yet the effects of both have long-range implications on policy, not only in reference to the structure of compensation, but also to productivity, retirement, and faculty morale (see the following section, "Equity in Compensation").

Most recently, hiring practices have tended to have the greatest disruptive power in preserving compensation systems tied closely to rank. Not only is competition becoming more of a factor in decisions about hiring; the collective process of determining rank and salary in academe is somewhat unusual and tends to hinder progress toward equity between ranks. Unlike many civil service or step-salary plans, most schemes to determine faculty salary in practice are full of overlaps and inconsistencies based on internal and external market factors. It happens because colleges and universities tend to fund individuals rather than positions. When a person retires in a position-based system in business, for example, someone else is advanced into that salary position, who in turn is replaced by someone else on down the line. Academe has no automatic replacement or chain of promotion into the full professorship when a senior faculty member retires. Instead, a senior faculty member is usually replaced by a new, junior faculty member, thereby eroding the salary base for all those remaining in their positions (Hansen 1986).

Compensation can be used apart from reliance on rank to reward status and prestige. At institutions with collective bargaining agreements, for example, seniority has long been a basic component in the salary structure for faculty (Begin 1979; Lee 1989). At some institutions, one approach to rewarding seniority is awarding longevity increases to all faculty in an effort to acknowledge progressive growth in experience (Kasper 1986). This approach to rewarding seniority might well seem appropriate given the nature of collegiate practices affecting promotion and tenure. The longer a professor serves at an institution using this system of reward for seniority, the greater the level of compensation, because of the perception that a senior faculty member is (or should be) "worth more" than a junior person. Long-standing professors have presumably paid their dues, provide much service to and for the institution, and socialize and train the newer faculty. As a result, faculty would expect to see, on average, those with higher rank and/or more years of institutional service receiving larger salaries than more junior, less experienced colleagues. Indeed, many pay scales are set on the premise that higher ranks are worth more to an institution. A recent national study of faculty across institutional types found that, on average, institutional seniority has a positive effect on salary but only through eight to 14 years of service; after that point, years spent at one institution (as a faculty member) have minimal effect on increasing salaries (Fairweather 1992). The actual break point in benefits from seniority is somewhat longer at comprehensive universities and liberal arts colleges, continuing through 20 or more years of service.

Although rewarding seniority sounds reasonable, a dilemma exists with using compensation for this purpose because if the process "works," one-half to three-quarters of an institution's full-time academic budget can be consumed by paying senior faculty, based primarily on the fact that they have long institutional relationships. The portrayal of the inverted professorial pyramid, in which the number of full professors exceeds the combined number of faculty in other ranks (Hacker 1992), has potentially serious consequences for practices of compensation. These circumstances are not alleviated by removing the ceiling on retirement, thereby allowing some of the highest-paid faculty to continue employment indefinitely. Across institutional type, colleges and universities face difficulties recruiting and retaining more junior faculty as a result of the dollars for compensation tied up in large numbers of senior faculty (Hacker 1992).

Many authors have suggested an argument contrary to these findings (see, e.g., Annual Report 1988; Bowen and Schuster 1986; Hamermesh 1988; Kasper 1988): that the effectiveness of rewarding seniority has been complicated by changes in the structures of compensation, the pool of qualified faculty, the erosion of base salaries caused by market influences and competition, and the introduction of the powerful ethos of merit-based salaries. Often the result for senior faculty is not increased salary but higher levels of salary compression. Evidence is growing of larger salary increases for new assistant professors than for continuing senior faculty or even for continuing assistant professors (Kasper 1988), resulting in a negative tenure slope that theoretically corrects itself after tenure. Bearing in mind the different effects of merit increases added to base salaries and percentage versus dollar increases, the compensation slope might not be easily remedied after tenure and promotion. An examination of distinctions within disciplines found that differences in salary associated with rank have expanded in lower-paying fields and compressed in those higher-paying fields where salaries grew quickly in the 1980s (Hamermesh 1988). The influence of the labor market is a significant factor in both compensation expansion and compression in that study.

A decade of comparisons shows that the salary levels of faculty who had been teaching 20 years were still below their levels in 1970–71, even after being adjusted for inflation,

representing a growth rate of less than 1 percent per year (Annual Report 1990, 1991). This discouraging statistic comes despite salary recovery during the 1980s and at a time when more junior faculty (newer assistant and associate professors) have experienced improvement in real salary. Compression, in its many facets, can leave senior faculty dispirited, feeling they have played faithfully by old institutional rules and are now faced with changing reward structures based on new activities and institutional priorities (Bowen and Schuster 1986). The effects of such changes, especially on those faculty who are still active and productive but who can never catch up economically, can be debilitating.

Even within the press of environmental factors, certain alternatives are at hand for rewarding seniority, service, and productivity. Institutional policy makers are looking to creative approaches that encompass a broader definition of compensation than just salary. Sabbatical programs, study leaves of absence, faculty development and renewal programs, and variation in teaching assignments are just a few of the creative options (Bowen and Schuster 1986; Clark and Lewis 1985; Wheeler and Schuster 1990). While none of these suggestions are new to academe, they are usually associated with the basic faculty contract and are not necessarily seen as rewards for seniority. When the traditional reward structures are effective with junior faculty (Baldwin and Krotseng 1985), monetary and nonmonetary perquisites like those mentioned could provide more appropriate incentives for senior faculty whose career options and interests have changed. What is needed is a structure that fairly rewards associate and full professors by providing meaningful incentives for different stages of faculty careers. As policy planners look for structures that will foster productivity and a sense of purpose and value in their senior faculty, broader and more creative definitions of compensation could be the order of the day.

Rewarding Productivity throughout a Career

The discussion of rewarding seniority and the need to carefully evaluate the effectiveness of reward structures is in part based on the assumption that faculty perceive the institutional reward structure differently throughout their careers. Put another way, do faculty needs and values (the crux of effective reward structures) vary throughout the professorial career? Given the static nature of most institutional compensation systems, it would appear that policy planners believe faculty values are constant over a career as well as in institutional time, as many colleges and universities have done little to alter historically embedded compensation structures. Research on faculty over the last decade, however, has shed new light on what most faculty already know: Internal and external rewards for faculty differ in primacy over their careers (Baldwin 1979, 1990; Baldwin and Blackburn 1981; Baldwin and Krotseng 1985; Blackburn 1985; Clark and Lewis 1985; El-Khawas 1991; Finkelstein 1984a; McKeachie 1979; Schuster, Wheeler, et al. 1990; H. Tuckman 1979; Tuckman and Belisle 1987).

The impact of various compensation structures on faculty throughout their careers can be examined in several ways. One approach is the use of development theory to examine faculty careers. In the early period of a career, faculty are primarily occupied with professional self-definition and acceptance by peers. They might be preoccupied with accomplishing those tasks perceived to lead to these objectives as defined by institution and discipline (Baldwin 1990). Becoming an effective teacher, establishing a coherent line of research and scholarship, and establishing an institutional and/or national reputation are common agendas for junior faculty across institutions throughout the probationary period. Colleges and universities that rely on compensation structures based on rewarding traditional definitions of productivity find their incentives particularly effective with junior faculty (Baldwin and Krotseng 1985; H. Tuckman 1979; Tuckman and Belisle 1987). Faculty at lower ranks, presumably at early stages in their careers, are more greatly influenced by and receptive to traditional institutional incentives and rewards for productivity. Compensation structures based on rewarding productivity strongly favor those with entire careers ahead of them (Baldwin and Krotseng 1985). This cause-and-effect relationship makes sense when we remember that, for an untenured developing faculty member, the traditional institutional compensation policy provides not only financial rewards for a junior faculty member's productivity but also opportunities for promotion, tenure, and future career options in relatively short order (six to ten years), thus satisfying the primary developmental objectives of this stage of a career (H. Tuckman 1979; Tuckman and Belisle 1987).

Faculty in midcareer, usually associate or newer full professors, often feel established in their profession and in their institution and feel a certain mastery of their work, having met standards for tenure and promotion (Bowen and Schuster 1986; Hall 1986). This stage of a career might be a period of maximum productivity according to traditional academic definitions. If so, those in midcareer might continue to reap the benefits of an institutional compensation system based on productivity, and some might be interested in preserving the pay for a structure that compensates performance. If midcareer proves not to be a period of maximum productivity, however, faculty might favor alternate forms of compensation that more accurately reflect changes in work load. Regardless of the level of activity, it is quite likely that midcareer faculty will reexamine personal value systems and professional concerns. Balance between work and personal roles becomes more important at this developmental stage (Cross 1984; Hall 1986), as does defining a sense of future orientation within or apart from one's current institution.

As part of this process, faculty might pursue changes in professional activity—pursuing new lines of research, taking on administrative responsibilities and interdisciplinary teaching assignments, or developing new teaching methods and curricula. Sabbatical leaves are often available to midcareer faculty for retooling and refocusing their career objectives. It is also true that, at many institutions, such opportunities are allocated based on traditional measures of previous productivity in research and for research activities more than instructional projects or career adjustments (Baldwin 1990; McKeachie 1979). Here the dilemma of the purpose of the reward system comes into play. Is it reward for past performance or incentive for new activity? What is merit versus worth in institutional terms?

On the one hand, compensation benefits like sabbatical leaves are subject to the same assessment dilemma as merit pay (a reliance on quantitative, easily comparable criteria) and could bypass the very group of faculty that could most be rewarded and assisted. On the other hand, colleges and universities that have made serious commitments to faculty development programs as mechanisms for enhancing careers and faculty activity have developed alternative leave programs and opened the criteria by which sabbaticals are awarded so that the long-standing relationships between faculty members and their institution can continue to be mutually productive (Centra 1985; Seldin 1990).

Those in late careers challenge the compensation structure in different ways. In those institutions that do not reward seniority as discussed, senior faculty are often removed from access to traditional forms of compensation. They might be beyond the point of maximum productivity or might be involved in different kinds of activities from those encouraged by the reward system. Yet they continue to make valuable contributions based on knowledge and experience (Baldwin 1990). Unfortunately, most compensation structures do not respond to changes in the kinds of professional activities or value systems that senior faculty experience. For instance, senior faculty might be more interested in teaching than their more junior colleagues, even though teaching is often rewarded far less (a viewpoint held by 74 percent of faculty at four-year institutions and 96 percent at two-year institutions [El-Khawas 1991]). Senior faculty also remain active in scholarship and scholarly pursuits, although the rate of productivity might have dropped some and the definition of scholarship broadened over time. They might also be less likely than others to receive external research funding (El-Khawas 1991). If compensation systems are designed to reward productivity and measures of productivity continue to favor research and publications, then, again, senior faculty might not be adequately rewarded for their forms of activity.

Recruitment and Retention
Salaries and wages usually account for the largest single element in a college or university budget, amounting to approximately 70 percent of a typical institutional budget. Although faculty salaries rose during 1980 to 1987, they did not keep pace with increases realized by comparable professional groups (Hansen 1988a). Increases in salaries were also unevenly distributed across institutional type and sector during the 1980s. Some colleges and universities have raised salaries to compete effectively with the private sector and with each other. For other institutions where faculty salaries continue to lag, the choice for policy makers is to follow suit or face a serious disadvantage in replacing faculty and retaining the ones they have. The dilemma is compounded by different effects of compensation levels across rank, discipline, and institutional type (Ehrenberg, Kasper, and Rees 1991). In one study, level of compensation had a greater impact on retention rates of assistant and associate faculty but not on full profes-

sors. At the same time, the study showed that the effect of salary on lower ranks became even greater as institutions became less selective and more oriented toward teaching. Public and private institutional control also affected the strength of the relationship between retention and level of compensation, making the use of compensation as a primary factor in recruitment and retention a complicated task at best. Thus, hiring and retention are two principal preoccupations of administrative officers responsible for faculty resources. These administrators must keep one eye on the marketplace outside the college and the other on the internal climate where morale and productivity are the watchwords.

It is also possible to look at the impact and value of institutional compensation structures over faculty careers through studies of retention and attrition, where evidence suggests that faculty will leave a position for different reasons over the course of a career. Some studies show that salary is the single most important determinant of faculty departures, regardless of rank or career stage (Annual Report 1990). Other studies suggest a combination of factors that vary across one's career, many of which cannot be altered by policies and practices affecting compensation. For instance, in one study dismissal or denial of tenure accounted for one-half of assistant professors' departures (Burke 1987), while resignations of assistant professors were attributed with equal frequency to intellectual isolation and intellectual incompatibility with senior colleagues. Salary was indicated less frequently as a primary reason for leaving the institution. Another study confirms the importance of nonmonetary factors in the junior faculty's perceptions of success or failure (Whitt 1991). Other studies of assistant professors support the idea that aspects of the academic career apart from compensation greatly influence the decision to leave an institution (see, e.g., Amey 1991; Johnsrud 1992; Sorcinelli 1988), thereby relegating to secondary status the use of compensation as a strategy to retain assistant professors.

As faculty move through midlife transitions, intrinsic rewards apart from traditional compensation systems, such as closer relationships with students and colleagues, take on a primary role in determining morale and satisfaction (McKeachie 1979). Similarly, prestigious opportunities afforded senior faculty as a result of established reputations, such as national speeches, international committee responsibilities, and invited essays, might take away from time spent on traditional teaching and research. Opportunities to participate in and be rewarded for such relationships and activities become central factors in faculty decisions to stay with or leave an institution.

A more recent study found that two-thirds of the associate and full professors in the study ranked "personal factors" as very important reasons for leaving an institution (Weiler 1985). The two most frequently cited personal factors were relationships with colleagues and career changes, neither of which could be altered through compensation systems, including money for retention. It is important to note, however, that a salary increase or the potential for an increase was an important factor among many of the same respondents. Increase in income might have been a function of extrainstitutional factors like consulting or spousal income, however, rather than simply an increase in base salary. Relationships with colleagues, lack of support for research, and hostility in the department were key reasons in another study in senior faculty members' decisions to leave an institution, while salary rarely served as a motivator (Burke 1988). Other evidence suggests that senior faculty often move to other institutions to assume senior administrative responsibilities, such as deanships, vice presidencies, and presidencies (Annual Report 1990). Again, increased salary might come as a result of increased responsibilities, yet faculty at this level report the change of position is the key to the decision to leave, not compensation per se.

Variation in reasons to leave an institution occur across disciplines as well as rank (Bowen and Schuster 1986; Hansen 1985; H. Tuckman 1979). Differences in gender might also exist (Amey 1991; Barbezat 1988; Bowen and Schuster 1986; Witt and Lovrich 1988). It is too easy to assume that compensation alone will keep a faculty member at a given institution, although it might play into the decision to leave. At the same time, increased salary is often the only thing chairs or deans present to counter a job offer. Policy planners and decision makers need to recognize the complexity of faculty careers and how circumstances and priorities in values change over time to develop effective personnel policies—of which compensation is only a part.

The other issue of cost and policy related to recruitment and retention is benefits. Some institutions estimate that a yearly growth in salaries of about 1.5 percent is necessary to

It is too easy to assume that compensation alone will keep a faculty member at a given institution, although it might play into the decision to leave.

keep up with growth in wages nationally, with an additional 0.5 percent needed to keep pace with steadily rising costs for benefits (Warner 1988), which not only includes mandated obligations like social security, medical insurance, and retirement, but also a growing demand for new benefit programs that range from daycare to wellness clinics. As the faculty diversifies nationally in terms of age, race, gender, and other characteristics, a recruiting- and retention-minded college or university will try to add attractive nonsalary items to its repertoire of incentives.

Retention and counteroffers

Not every college or university has an institutionwide policy regarding counteroffers (efforts to retain faculty through compensation). Often, these decisions are left to deans or division heads to develop and implement based on broad institutional guidelines and more specific needs of a unit.

A study of faculty on two campuses found that securing an offer of employment from another institution had a significant effect on compensation (Matier 1990), regardless of whether the offer was accepted or not. When firm offers are on the table, an institution often tries to meet the market demand by matching the offer in an attempt to retain the faculty member. Such use of compensation to retain faculty, however, can also be interpreted as a "viable" mechanism for obtaining increases (Matier 1990). To discourage such perceptions, institutions might set guidelines for how deans or division heads may proceed in addressing counteroffers. For instance, the University of Kansas College of Liberal Arts and Sciences set down a comprehensive plan for addressing counteroffers that is presumed to assist faculty, department chairs, and the college office in making decisions about faculty with offers from other institutions (Univ. of Kansas 1990). Without overly constraining those involved in negotiation, the guidelines dispel the myth of using counteroffers to get increased salaries and try to appease issues of morale that might develop within and across disciplines.

When developed as a strategy to retain faculty, counteroffers should be negotiated to include the relevant circumstances of the individual and might or might not focus exclusively on salary. Individual factors (rather than strictly salary) were the keys to the ultimate decision to stay at or leave an institution in another study (Weiler 1985). Therefore, to be effec-

tive, "policies" about counteroffers need to use a broader definition of compensation.

Recruiting stars and targets of opportunity

It is difficult to find documentation of the use of compensation for recruiting faculty "stars," although intuitively faculty
and administrators know that this practice periodically occurs.
Some discussion exists about the ability of various institutions
to compete with each other and with the private sector to
recruit and retain top-quality faculty. As a result of faculty
members' attraction to perceived higher-quality academic
institutions and the ability of those institutions to offer attractive compensation packages, a clustering of faculty stars is
likely in a few places (Freeman 1979).

Sometimes the practice of hiring stars is for purposes of
increasing institutional visibility and perceived reputation.
Tucker (1987) criticizes the practice, especially when the stars
are not "true" academics even if they do have special talents
or skills. He suggests that when deans or senior administrators
bring expert practitioners, such as public commentators, onto
college campuses as faculty, they run the risk of undermining
faculty governance, academic standards, and the ability to
equitably compensate faculty who already are in the system.
Other problems are associated with keeping stars' salaries
comparatively higher than other faculty members' salaries
across the institution or in comparable institutions. Although
many colleges and universities cannot compete with salaries
in the private sector, academic parity could suffice in retaining
quality faculty.

Other references to using compensation for "targets of
opportunity" focus more on the effect of such practices on
faculty morale (Bowen and Schuster 1986; Burgan 1988;
Tucker 1987). It is possible for star faculty to positively affect
departmental climates, to bring research dollars into an institution, allowing for the hiring of graduate students, and to
bring prestige and diversity to the campus. More notice is
given to the potential negative impacts of certain practices
in hiring stars, however, especially those related to a tiered
system of rewards. Those brought in at above-average salaries
might also be awarded additional travel money and opportunities, reduced teaching and advising loads, and freedom
from departmental and institutional committee work (Burgan
1988)—leading to increased loads for other faculty without

additional compensation and quite often to a feeling of resentment. Such practices of compensation can also result in the increased hiring of part-time faculty to handle the slack in the traditional academic area of the star, again making the practice questionable from the perspective of compensation.

Another issue related to using compensation to recruit special types of faculty concerns monies designated for recruiting faculty from underrepresented groups, such as women and minorities (Menges and Exum 1983). When allocated by state legislatures for use in public institutions, these monies might have specific guidelines attached that do not necessarily correspond with an institution's needs but are designed to increase the representation of these groups. Such funds might be particularly vulnerable to government cutbacks and could also negatively affect monies allocated for regular salary increments (Burgan 1988). Nevertheless, many institutions use a form of such strategies as a way to increase the number of women and minorities and to stimulate broader definitions of talent and need.

Supplemental Compensation

The latest decade of no growth and even decline in real salaries has pressured faculty into seeking additional sources of income (Marsh and Dillon 1980). As many as 85 percent of faculty report some supplemental income (Bowen and Schuster 1986; Boyer and Lewis 1985), though the amount of income, opportunity, and type of activity varies considerably across fields and disciplines.

Several sources of supplemental income are usually available within a college or university, most of which are accepted if not encouraged by administrators and policy makers. Compensation for additional teaching assignments is very common, whether it be for overload, summer arrangements, or teaching in continuing education. Other internal sources include assuming administrative responsibilities, developing new courses and curricula, and contracting for summer research (Silander 1983). Overall, additional teaching is the most frequently cited source of internally generated extra compensation (Bowen and Schuster 1986).

Perhaps less acceptable to society but more lucrative for faculty are compensated activities outside the institution. Faculty often mention income from research, extrainstitutional teaching, royalties, lecture fees, sales of art work, artistic performances, and consulting as important sources of supplemental compensation. Many of these sources, however, pose numerous ethical questions, societal and institutional concerns, and issues about faculty professional development.

Many people no longer view faculty as underpaid professionals whose commitment to academe reflects nonmonetary values. Societal mistrust is growing toward fee-for-service faculty activities that might or might not be supported by actual faculty behaviors. On the other hand, many of these outside activities are expected of faculty as they become established members of their profession. The external orientation brings prestige to the home institution and is a measure of individual reputation and acclaim (Bowen and Schuster 1986).

The crux of the issue centers on faculty work time and who owns it (Clark and Dillon 1982). In many circumstances, it is difficult for faculty to earn supplemental income without using institutional resources in some way. The use of materials, equipment, and support personnel (secretaries, graduate students, and phones, for example) causes critics to question whether the institution should not receive some return on its investment, perhaps in the form of time or percentage of income from royalties and consulting fees. Other issues arise like the possible neglect of students and other institutional responsibilities as a result of outside activities (Yuker 1984). Some are concerned about abuses of academic freedom and conflicts of interest, particularly when faculty are teaching at a competing institution or when they are involved in certain professionally related business ventures. A question also arises about property rights on discoveries and patents for those involved in research (Boyer and Lewis 1984; Clark and Dillon 1982; Goldstein 1987).

Research on faculty professional activities shows evidence to counter many of these societal concerns. Studies have demonstrated that although the number of faculty members involved in outside activities has increased, most faculty record earnings accounting for less than 15 percent of their base salaries. A large proportion of faculty earn money only during the summer break in a nine-month contract (Marsh and Dillon 1980). Abuses of facilities and personnel are rare. Faculty who earn supplemental incomes tend to do more research and are no less institutionally active than their colleagues. Their activities generally complement faculty responsibilities, including the ability to incorporate the results of and applications of real-work theories and hypotheses into the classroom (Boyer and Lewis 1985). By providing the opportunity for testing and research in noncollegiate settings and by keeping abreast of the latest needs and developments in the field, involvement in outside professional activities allows for the continuing education of faculty members. Colleges and universities are often unable to provide similar opportunities for development themselves.

The institution also receives significant benefits of a faculty member's involvement in outside activities. By permitting outside activities to supplement the base salary, institutions might be better able to attract and retain high-quality faculty. Faculty activities help build the professional reputation of a given department or university and represent a commitment of service to the community at large. Particularly important to research, outside activities provide institutional access to the private sector, government contracts, and foundation monies that otherwise might be less available (Boyer and Lewis 1984, 1985; Dillon and Bane 1980; Yuker 1984).

The emergence and careful development of research partnerships between academic institutions and the private sector are examples of constructive ways to facilitate extrainstitutional research in a way that mutually benefits the institution and the individual. When the development of partnerships is seen in light of compensation policies and practices, it allows an institution flexibility to provide incentives to retain faculty without necessarily increasing base salaries (Goldstein 1987). Access to state-of-the-art facilities, research funding, and additional graduate students are attractive aspects of creative resource partnerships that could enhance institutional compensation policies in the future. The emergence of entrepreneurial relationships between some faculty and their universities, such as shared ventures with shared profits in biotechnology and other patent-rich fields, is already forcing the development of new guidelines for employment and compensation (Fairweather 1988).

In working with the issues surrounding compensation for outside activities, policy makers might need to develop models that more accurately assess the relationship between the outside activities and the faculty member's internal responsibilities. The relationship should reflect the institution's mission and objectives and therefore cannot be universally defined. Some more comprehensive and carefully designed institutional policies establish clear accountability for faculty over a wide range of concerns (Clark and Dillon 1982). Yet a fine distinction exists between accountability and infringement on academic freedom. Conscientious policy making accompanied by the faculty's professional self-regulation is the goal. Organizational structures, roles, and relationships should be clearly and carefully defined to achieve the optimum balance between the need for faculty autonomy and institutional accountability.

Summary
Developing appropriate personnel policies must begin by clearly defining existing salary and benefit policies, particularly focusing on the criteria used to award salaries and structure compensation (Braskamp, Muffo, and Langston 1978; Lawler 1990). While many institutions now have routine policies in writing, others still do not. Embedded within all routine considerations of hiring, promotion, and merit are concerns for balance and flexibility. The balance might involve differences in salary between junior and senior faculty, but it might as likely involve concerns for differences among departments and colleges. Flexibility could take the form of responding to a professor's job offer from another institution or redressing institutional inequities attributable to differences in gender or race. The complement to careful policy making is the development of a reciprocal relationship between institutional policies and faculty needs and integrity (Clark and Dillon 1982). Achieving equitable and humane structures of compensation is no easy or automatic task, and it is likely to grow even more complex in the years ahead.

EQUITY IN COMPENSATION

Equity generally is a central concept in pay systems. Ideally, equity means "attempting to ensure fair pay treatment for all participants . . . [and] designing pay systems that recognize both employee contributions (e.g., offering higher pay for greater performance or greater experience or training) and employee needs (e.g., providing a living wage or health care insurance)" (Milkovich and Newman 1990, p. 8). Inequitable compensation policies and practices can result in poor use of human resources, frustration and discord, and lower institutional productivity.

Compensation policies and practices are underwritten by several important federal laws and regulations. The Equal Pay Act of 1963, for example, amends in four sentences the provisions for minimum wage of the Fair Labor Standards Act of 1938 prohibiting sex discrimination in jobs where differences in performance are not significant in determining pay. Executive Order 11246 (as amended by Executive Order 11375), issued in 1972 as part of the higher education guidelines of the Department of Health, Education, and Welfare, also mandates that men and women be paid equally for equal work and compensated equally in terms of benefits. Although not originally included under the earlier laws, colleges and universities were added subsequently in the Education Amendments of 1972 (Title IX). The amendments ensure that executive, managerial, and professional workers are included, with the intent of comparing jobs, not people. These guidelines also mandated affirmative action plans for all federal contractors, including colleges and universities.

Title VII of the Civil Rights Act of 1964 prohibits discrimination on the basis of sex, race, color, religion, or national origin in any condition of employment, including hiring, firing, promotion, transfer, compensation, and admission to training programs. Title VII was amended in 1972 and 1978 to include employees of government and educational institutions when they employ more than 15 people.

The Pregnancy Discrimination Act of 1978 is also an amendment to Title VII of the Civil Rights Act. Employers are required to extend to pregnant employees or spouses of employees the same disability and medical benefits provided other employees or spouses of employees.

In addition, the Age Discrimination in Employment Act of 1967 (amended in 1978) makes nonfederal employees between the ages of 40 and 70 a protected class relative to

The amendments ensure that executive, managerial, and professional workers are included, with the intent of comparing jobs, not people.

their treatment in pay, benefits, and other personnel actions. The act is intended "to promote employment of older persons on their ability rather than age; to prohibit arbitrary age discrimination in employment; [and] to help employers and workers find ways of meeting problems arising from the impact of age on employment." Subsequently, amendments passed in 1986 strengthened the act's power. Beginning in January 1994, tenured faculty are entitled to remain in their jobs as long as they are able to perform their responsibilities.

In 1981, the U.S. Supreme Court resolved some of the confusion between the coverage provided in the Equal Pay Act and Title VII of the Civil Rights Act when it held that Title VII incorporated the affirmative defenses of the Equal Pay Act but is not limited to the equal-pay-for-equal-work formula of that act. In essence, the laws were designed to prohibit discrimination in two forms: disparate treatment in which different standards are applied to different individuals or groups with a clear intent to discriminate, and disparate impact in which the same standards have different consequences for individuals or groups. In the latter case, the legal tests focus on general statistical impact rather than the presence of discriminatory intent (Milkovich and Newman 1990).

The federal laws and regulations and various state statutes have attempted to put a legal foundation under the idea of equity. Still, considerable controversy surrounds the idea and its application to various individuals and groups within academe. Three areas relating to inequity in salaries have been the focus of most research on equity in higher education: "studies [that] document the existence of salary discrimination; studies [that] attempt to explain (and occasionally to justify) salary inequities; and analyses of various methodological tools used to prove or disprove the existence of salary discrimination on a particular campus" (Lee and Olswang 1985, p. 235).

Gender

Studies of the existence of salary discrimination in academe mostly concern sex or gender. Why? Because study after study since the 1960s discovered a persistent salary gap between men and women faculty at every rank, in virtually every field, and in every type of institution (see table 1). Affirmative action policies have had an impact on the hiring of women, but salary and rank are still inequitably awarded (Loeb, Ferber, and Lowry 1978; Reskin et al. 1992). Early research (H. Tuck-man 1979) found that male faculty members on average earned $1,143 more than female faculty of similar rank and productivity. Others found a persistent salary gap of 11 percent (Gordon, Morton, and Braden 1974). An examination of national data for 1968, 1977, and 1983 found salary gaps of 11.5 to 17.7 percent, 5.5 to 11.5 percent, and 19 percent, respectively, in favor of male faculty members (Barbezat 1987b; see also Bayer and Astin 1975; Fox 1985; Sandler 1979). Most recently, data from the National Center for Educational Statistics's National Survey of Postsecondary Education Faculty showed that "women were consistently underpaid compared with their male counterparts" (Fairweather 1992, p. 43), an average of about $11,180.

TABLE 1

AVERAGE FACULTY SALARIES FOR MEN AND WOMEN BY RANK, 1992-93

	All		Public		Private, Independent		Church-related	
	Men	Women	Men	Women	Men	Women	Men	Women
Institutions with Academic Ranks								
Professor	$60,620	$53,460	$59,240	$52,900	$70,180	$59,970	$52,430	$46,720
Associate professor	44,990	41,830	44,810	41,840	48,070	44,410	41,940	38,650
Assistant professor	38,010	35,080	38,110	35,310	40,300	36,390	34,600	32,710
Instructor	28,570	26,960	28,670	27,010	29,340	27,750	27,350	26,200
Lecturer	33,310	29,110	32,610	28,570	37,240	32,150	31,410	27,390
Institutions without Academic Ranks								
All	41,980	32,080	42,110	32,160	28,660	27,760	26,180	25,100

Note: Figures cover full-time members of the instructional staff except those in medical schools and are based on 2,147 institutions. Salaries are adjusted to a standard nine-month work year.
Source: AAUP, cited in *Chronicle of Higher Education,* 14 April 1993, p. A22. Reprinted with permission.

The rank and tenure system on which faculty compensation is based adds to the problem of gaps in salary and confounds accurate inter- and intrainstitutional analysis. Women are found primarily at lower ranks, including an increasing number of non-tenure-track positions, and at lower paying types of institutions, particularly nonresearch universities (Linnell 1979; Silander 1983). They are not promoted at the same rate as male faculty, so they do not have similar access to the compensation and benefits associated with rank, tenure, and seniority (Sandler 1979). The accumulative disadvantages women faculty experience in other areas of their professional lives apparently apply to their compensation as well (Clark and Corcoran 1986).

These national surveys are mirrored by countless institutional studies (e.g., at Pennsylvania State University, Princeton University, the University of Wisconsin System, Ohio State University, the University of Michigan) that have found virtually similar salary gaps between men and women faculty (Koch and Chizmar 1976; Spector 1989). While the salary gap appeared to narrow in the late 1970s (Barbezat 1988), it began to widen again in the late 1980s. What are possible explanations for this persistent salary gap?

Explanations of the salary gap

Scholars have sought to employ three different theories—discrimination theory, human capital theory, and supply-and-demand theory (Blackburn and Holbert 1987; McElrath 1992; White 1990). *Discrimination theory* proposes that gaps in wages are the result of overt discrimination against women by individual institutions. For example, if an institution deliberately treats a female faculty member as a "deviant case" by paying her consistently below her male colleagues, or if a department devalues a woman's research or teaching because it is related to women (although it is similar in quantity and quality with research conducted by men in the department), such cases would probably fit a claim of discrimination. For the most part, such overt forms of sex discrimination appear to have been eliminated from the policies, if not always the practices, of colleges and universities. More hidden rationales, however, couched in the language of market-based decisions or condoned by the culture of society, are coming under increasing criticism from several perspectives, including comparable worth.

A second perspective, *human capital theory,* suggests that men and women differ in their productive capacity and that these differences account for salary gaps between men and women. According to this argument, men bring more labor value to the workplace in terms of their skills, qualifications, and attitudes and so are offered higher salaries (Blackburn and Holbert 1987; Finkelstein 1984a; Freeman 1976). Some of the reasons given for the apparent gap in wages are that academic women tend to be younger, hold fewer degrees, have fewer years of service, and, most important, have produced less (Johnson and Stafford 1974). One study that attempted to probe a version of human capital theory to explain the gap accounted for 22 percent of the variance in men's and women's salaries through such variables as numbers of articles published, age, level of degree, years of continuous service at the present institution, and time spent in academe (Bayer and Astin 1975). Other studies that have tried to explore these variables in depth and with numerous statistical controls, however, tend to show that women with the same credentials, years of service, and so on are still paid less than comparable male colleagues (Cole 1979), leading at least one researcher to invoke Galton's Paradox: "How can it be that with qualifications held constant women receive less salary and with salary held constant women are less qualified?" (Pezzullo and Brittingham 1979, p. 22).

Several scholars (e.g., Fox 1981; Szafran 1984; White 1990) have explored this apparent paradox through close examination of the structure of academic employment, and one found that "women lose and men gain not so much from the way pay is allocated but from the way initial assignments and promotions are distributed" (Szafran 1984, p. 24). In fact, women tend to be located in lower-paying fields, such as health, social work, and education, tend to be located in lower ranks, and tend to be promoted more slowly. Conversely, "men tend to hold high-level administrative, research, and faculty positions and tend to be located in business, technical, and medical professional schools and the natural and social science departments . . ." (Fox 1981, p. 82). Thus, salary gaps between men and women could be attributed to properties of the location or structure of employment as well as the employee's characteristics.

Thus, an underlying question is posed: To what extent has the institution used a principle of equity in the distribution of male and female faculty into favorable or unfavorable employment locations? If women have been prevented from receiving high-level posts or not hired into certain lucrative fields despite qualifications, then it is the employer who is the source of the resulting difference in salary, not any inherent lack of qualifications on the part of the female faculty member.

Human capital theory maintains that rational bases exist for the differential distribution of pay to males and females in academe. The decentralized structure and the tradition of departmental autonomy, however, that characterize universities in particular, make it especially challenging to discern what can be attributed to organizational factors and what can be attributed to the characteristics of female and male faculty members. Principles of equity can be invoked at the institutional level, only to be breached or abrogated at the departmental level, unless various controls and monitoring devices are put in place to ensure conformity to expected policies and procedures.

A final conundrum in considering the weight and value of human capital theory as it applies to academe concerns the issue of qualifications, specifically performance. Performance, or achievement as it has been labeled, is "not merely a criterion of reward . . . [but] rather . . . has intrinsic value for the very activity and goals of the institution" (Fox 1981, pp. 81–82). Faculty members accord great legitimacy to the criteria, evaluations, and rewards provided by their profession (Fox 1981). They might tend to regard the outcomes based on such criteria and evaluations as similarly equitable and legitimate because they tend to attribute those rewards to individual performance rather than institutional structures. With respect to gender, "academic salary forms dual reward structures . . . similar in the dominance of achievement variables, yet different in payment level and structure for men compared with women" (Fox 1981, p. 81). Further, a proportional salary advantage accrues to men over time (Barbezat 1987b). Only as patterns of discrepant rewards are revealed and only as the structural nature of discriminatory treatment is made public have academics begun to realize the intricate and sophisticated nature of their disparate employment conditions.

A third competing theoretical explanation for sex discrimination in salary concerns *supply and demand.* This theory suggests that salaries are determined by the relative supply and demand of people occupying jobs. When an excess of labor exists, salaries are driven down, and when a scarcity of labor exists, salaries increase (White 1990). According to advocates of this theory, women have tended to select less-well-paying occupations, but when they are part of scarce occupational groups, they tend to receive equally high salaries. Differences in salary occur as a result of market reactions to women's voluntary life choices, such as reduced hours and less training (Johnson and Stafford 1979). Further, differences could also be a factor of premarket discrimination that could have affected a woman's original choices with regard to career and/or discipline, thereby eventually leading to salary inequities based on market factors associated with various disciplines.

"Underutilization" is a word used to determine those situations when fewer women or minorities participate in a particular job group than would be reasonably expected based on their availability (Lindgren et al. 1984). The word came into use because academic employers were not conforming to the theory of supply and demand. In numerous hiring situations, in particular, institutions were not hiring women or minorities proportionate to their presence in the labor market and, in some cases, were failing to pay them equivalent high salaries based on their scarcity. In general, studies of underutilization point to an underlying criticism of the theory of supply and demand, namely, that academic employers have had the power to shape their policies and practices regarding hiring and remuneration to a considerable extent by ignoring issues of supply and demand when it suits them. The more prestigious the institution, the more able it is to use its discretion in recruitment and rewards (Smelser and Content 1980; Szafran 1984), which might explain why of all types of institutions, research universities remain the most discriminatory on the basis of sex in faculty pay and rank (Moore and Sagaria 1991).

Moreover, universities control the supply side of the equation as well. When they were not admitting women as students into fields like engineering, physics, and medicine, they virtually controlled the recruitment stream as well. Fortunately, many overt and covert quota systems have been eliminated from graduate programs, and many more women (and minorities) are finding places for graduate study.

Two other conditions could permit academic units to ignore various dimensions of supply and demand. When men and women are segregated into same-sex units, as they frequently are within a university or college, discrepant salary treatment might not be widely evident and so not recognized (Fox 1981). "Salary disparity between the sexes is more tenable when it is less apparent, and separation makes the sexes as well as the discrepant rewards less visible to each other" (p. 43). Thus, it might be easier to rationalize paying all of the nursing faculty, who might happen to be female, lower salaries than it is a particular female colleague within a mixed-sex department. Departments tend not to know what other departments or fields are being paid and might not even think it is relevant to know. Similarly, when salaries are kept extremely confidential, or even secret, it also becomes possible to ignore or override discrepant salary issues that favor male faculty members.

An early study identified several factors affecting women that tend to increase salary differentials over time (Tuckman and Tuckman 1976). Lack of opportunities for research, heavy teaching loads, advising and committee work, lack of support for scholarly work, and less mobility are negative contributors over which a woman might have little personal control and that might not resolve themselves easily in the academic workplace. "Salaries are relative and linked in a network of relationships. . . . The most exacting analyses of salaries cannot take into account the prior discrimination that leaves women at a disadvantage in what appears to be nondiscriminatory variables (degree, experience, publication) and other hidden conditions that differentially affect women in salary determination" (Pezzullo and Brittingham 1979, p. 10). Clearly the presentation of a pure supply-and-demand or market-driven rationale for the gap between men's and women's salaries is fraught with difficulties.

In the main, attempts to "prove" sex discrimination in salaries in academe have rested in case law rather than theory (Hendrickson and Lee 1983; LaNoue and Lee 1987). The courts have had to address a "threshold issue" as a framework for considering sex discrimination cases: the equality or comparability of faculty jobs (Lee and Olswang 1985). "The question is whether faculty positions are equal at all, or whether departmental and individual differences are too substantial to permit comparisons, for example, between an assistant professor of biochemistry and an assistant professor of physical education" (p. 236).

The Equal Pay Act and Title VII of the Civil Rights Act as amended contain a four-factor definition of what constitutes equal work: skill, effort, responsibility, and working conditions. Employers may not discriminate against a person on the basis of sex if that person's work meets the four-factor definition. Conversely, an employer may pay people differently if their work is different based on those four factors or on the basis of "other factors" related to the work itself. In academe, the "other factor" argument used for discrimination in pay often has been merit (Birnbaum 1979; Gray 1985). But as noted earlier, merit or achievement is not always as easy to discern as it might seem.

Nevertheless, as various observers have pointed out (e.g., Lee and Olswang 1985; Lindgren et al. 1984), plaintiffs who seek to bring charges of salary discrimination against universities and colleges have difficulty winning their suits in large part because of the burden of proof they must bear. A plaintiff or plaintiffs must show that he or she was paid less than a better-paid colleague for a job whose actual performance required substantially equal skill, effort, and responsibility. And, in addition, the plaintiff must also show that the difference in salary could not be attributed to one of the "affirmative defenses" allowed by law, including a "factor other than sex" (e.g., market or merit). Merit in particular is "an inclusive term that is presumed to depend on a variety of factors, including years of professional experience, quality of scholarly contribution, service, impact, and recognition" (Birnbaum 1979, p. 138).

To both discover possible salary discrimination on the basis of sex for institutional or research purposes and to "prove" it in a court of law entail an increasing reliance on statistical procedures. The following subsections briefly consider the nature and use of statistical procedures in cases involving equitable salaries.

Statistical procedures used in salary equity
Two principal methods have been used to establish salary discrimination statistically: pairing and regression analysis. The pairing or counterparting technique involves matching male and female faculty members on the basis of similar qualifications. While some smaller institutions have employed this method extensively, it is cumbersome in larger institutions. It is also difficult if the female faculty members have no male peers, which might be possible in predominately female fields (Braskamp, Muffo, and Langston 1978). The paired method can demonstrate that inequity exists, but it cannot demonstrate its extent because it is limited to case-by-case comparisons. When individuals are permitted to do their own pairing, they might select the most extreme cases to make their point. For institutions just getting started in examining whether they have instances of sex discrimination in salary, the pairing

method is a good first step, however (Pezzullo and Britting-ham 1979).

Regression analysis essentially makes every conceivable paired comparison. It is a technique that uses correlational measures on a set of variables called predictors that are presumed to have a direct relationship with the variable—in this case, salary. The purpose of the technique is to "estimate the salary of a white male of specified characteristics so as to compare the resulting estimate with the actual salary of a female or minority person with those characteristics" (Gray 1985, p. 34). Sex is not used as a variable because the purpose is to predict what a woman's salary would be if her salary were compensated the same as a man's. Numerous studies have used various versions of regression analysis, and numerous studies have critiqued the methods employed (see Pezzullo and Brittingham's *Salary Equity* [1979] for a presentation of several of these studies using different perspectives). Virtually all analysts acknowledge that the task of determining equitable salaries is especially complex in colleges and universities, because every institution has many individuals with the same title but widely differing expertise, expectations, and salaries (Barbezat 1987b; Braskamp, Muffo, and Langston 1978; Pezzullo and Brittingham 1979). Similarly, the courts in which suits are brought for adjudication face the task of discerning whether the statistical analyses accurately reflect the situation under consideration as well as the added burden of critiquing the analyses themselves (Finkelstein 1980).

Critics have pointed out several difficulties in the methodology from varying perspectives. Among the most common concerns or limitations is the concern that the so-called unbiased predictor variables could be "tainted" by unlawful practices at the time of hiring or promotion (Lee and Olswang 1985). Institutions might have knowingly or unknowingly engaged in inequitable practices when hiring women faculty, such as starting them at a lower salary than an equally qualified male, or they might have promoted women inequitably with the result that base salary or rank, which are presumed to be "unbiased," are in fact affected.

Rank in particular tends to be confounded with achievement factors that could be tainted by sex bias, including publication practices that are not sex blind to creation of working conditions that serve as barriers to scholarship or instructional achievements (Moore and Sagaria 1991). These circumstances are very difficult to prove over several years of a career in comparison to male colleagues, but they might still be present and related to the current condition and salary.

Another factor that confounds regression analysis is the relationship between academic discipline and sex. The numeric overrepresentation of women in certain traditionally female fields has to be established, and then the lower-than-average salaries of persons in that field have to be established, which in turn could be the result of broader societal views of the value of certain types of women's work compared to men's work. Such relationships are extremely difficult to disentangle factually and objectively, because they themselves are entangled in sex-based preconceptions.

A third stumbling block is the difficulty of stating qualitative differences in quantifiable terms. "Statistical studies attempt to predict salaries completely from a finite set of input variables even though most hiring and promotion policies place at least some, if not considerable, emphasis on hard-to-quantify attributes of the person being hired or promoted" (Pezzullo and Brittingham 1979, p. 8). However difficult it might be, all relevant variables must be included, because the regression technique assumes that differences in salary that are not explained by some predictor variable can be attributed to sex discrimination (Lee and Olswang 1985).

On the other hand, adding many potentially relevant variables is of marginal use (Gray and Scott 1980). "Most white males who have succeeded are relatively homogeneous so that knowing their salary and their experience indirectly tells as much about the other possible variables" (p. 176). Further, homogeneity is more pronounced in more prestigious universities so that regression analysis should be more accurate in a research university than in a community college that tends to have considerably more diverse faculty.

Flagging is a procedure some institutions use in conjunction with multiple regression as a means of addressing identified instances of salary discrimination. Flagging is the case-by-case examination of women who fall below the regression line to determine whether their salary is a result of "lack of merit" or true sex discrimination (Gray 1985). Flagging is a flawed remedy, however, as the process of asking women's cases to be evaluated by the same people who made the original decision assigning them to a lower salary is questionable. Moreover, the subjective nature of many of the factors that

Such relationships are extremely difficult to disentangle factually and objectively, because they themselves are entangled in sex-based preconceptions.

enter a determination of merit raises further difficulties. Finally, merely investigating the cases of women who fall below the regression line ignores the possibility that women who are above the line deserve rewards even higher than they presently receive. That is, regression is a technique to determine whether a pattern of sex bias presumably touches all women, not merely those who appear to have suffered the most. The sexism identified is not merely individual but pertains to the class of women in general. Hence, flagging, which focuses on individuals and potentially individual corrections, is not appropriate when it is a class of people—women—who are shown to have been affected (Gray 1985).

These arguments lead to two types of legal cases that have used regression analysis: class action suits and reverse discrimination suits. Class action suits have used the technique to show that the discriminatory practices have applied to all individuals similarly situated, not simply those who have brought the suit. Class action suits carry the presumption that "should the class plaintiffs prevail in court, the defendant college or university must provide the required relief to all members of the class, not just those individuals who initiated the suit" (Lee and Olswang 1985, p. 237).

Recent class action suits have resulted in sizable awards charged against institutions. The University of Minnesota, for example, came under a consent decree of $60 million plus $1.5 million in attorneys' fees. The City University of New York lost $60 million, and Montana State University faced a claim of $350,000 (Lee and Olswang 1985). Clearly, salary discrimination cases can mean extremely large financial consequences for universities and colleges.

Another type of case that uses regression analysis is reverse discrimination. In some instances, when the pay of women is adjusted in response to a claim of sex bias, men have claimed that they were paid less than women doing similar work, simply because they were men. At the University of Nebraska, for example, a new salary model was created with somewhat different variables. On the basis of the new model, 33 women were granted raises because their salaries were less than the amount computed by the model, but the university did not make comparable raises to 92 men whose salaries were also computed below the amount set by the model. The university was found in violation of the Equal Pay Act because it was held that rather than a one-time adjustment to eliminate the effects of past sex discrimination, which is allowable, the university was introducing a new model that should be applicable to all faculty, regardless of sex (Milkovich and Newman 1990).

A different methodological approach, causal modeling, was recently introduced to examine issues of gender equity (Smart 1991). The advantage of causal modeling is that the procedure "enables us to determine the direct effect of gender on academic rank and salary and to investigate how gender influences these achievements indirectly through intervening variables" (p. 514). The author deliberately examined variables used in various theoretical perspectives, such as human capital and structural functionalism. In this model, gender is entered as a single variable exogenous to the model.

With respect to his examination of the effect of gender on salary, Smart (1991) found that gender ranked third among 14 predictor variables, with only career age and professorial rank having larger total effects. The examination of the indirect effect of gender found that career age, academic rank, and the degree of male domination of academic disciplines were the primary variables through which gender indirectly influences salary. "Faculty members' gender is far more important to their academic rank and salary attainment than the kind of institution in which they work, their academic discipline, or the nature of work they perform in those institutions and disciplines" (Smart 1991, p. 522).

Comparable worth
Comparable worth is a relatively new concept in higher education, entering on the heels of salary equity. The idea originated in the women's movement because many salary differentials between similar if not equal jobs were suspected of being the result of sex bias and discrimination (Bergmann 1985). Today the concept is still associated with women but has more widespread implications (Milkovich and Newman 1990; Patten 1988). Claims citing comparable worth have to do with evaluating different jobs, rather than the same jobs, to see whether on the basis of general criteria comparability in compensation exists. In 1981, the U.S. Supreme Court ruled that it was not necessary for a plaintiff claiming salary discrimination to prove that she performed work exactly equal to that of men with whom she compared herself. While the decision was based on narrow procedural grounds, it has been

heralded as the opening case for comparable worth (Lee, Leslie, and Olswang 1987; Lee and Olswang 1985).

In a claim involving salary equity, a female professor might assert that she is paid less than similarly situated male colleagues in her department or college; in a claim involving comparable worth, that same woman would assert that she is paid less than a male colleague who is doing different work but of a type that requires similar credentials, skills, effort, or experience. The doctrine of comparable worth has significant implications for assessing the relative value of faculty trained in various disciplines (Lee and Olswang 1985).

Proponents of comparable worth argue that salaries based on market considerations are inherently discriminatory because the market reflects societal biases against women (Lee, Leslie, and Olswang 1987; Remick 1984). Opponents argue that the relationship between market factors and wages is too complex and that simply ignoring market realities will have greater negative effects on women, such as lower wages and higher unemployment. Moreover, academic salaries are and should be based on job performance, not job content (Lester 1974); that is, faculty members' contributions are the bases of different salaries. This point of view begs the question of whether the evaluation of the contributions is tainted by bias (Lee and Olswang 1985). Some unions to which some faculty might belong, such as the Communication Workers of America and the American Federation of State, County, and Municipal Employees, have actively supported comparable worth by negotiating pay increases based on it, lobbying for legislation, filing legal suits, and conducting educational programs for their members and the public about comparable worth (Milkovich and Newman 1990).

The application of the concept of comparable worth in academe has been difficult in part because of the differential influence of market factors on individual disciplines. As noted in earlier discussions, market factors have increasingly distinguished between the "worth" of various fields. One result of market influences is that departments place different emphases on research, teaching, and community service to the point that no generic definition of a faculty member seems to be apparent. The question becomes how to separate what an academic job is from what a faculty member does to have a basis for an analysis of comparable worth (Lee, Leslie, and Olswang 1987). Given the complexity of the issues, no quick fixes can address the issues of comparable worth and sex equity. Alternatives require long-term institutional investments and a method of adequately and accurately assessing academic positions.

Other gender-based compensation issues

Since the 1970s when sex discrimination was banned from most employment settings, higher education has come under increasing scrutiny for its policies of compensation and promotion. Numerous institutions have become involved in litigation because of alleged salary discrimination, both by individuals and by classes of female employees, resulting in greater efforts by institutions to review and clarify salary policies and practices as they affect women and causing faculty women to become more assertive in their demands for equitable compensations (Reskin et al. 1992).

Recently, concern for gender equity has turned to nonsalary areas of compensation, including fringe benefits. On the one hand, pressure is growing to provide gender-neutral benefits in health care, retirement, and other insurance. On the other hand, demand is growing for new programs and services tailored for women, such as expanded health coverage for maternity leaves and mammograms, and day-care centers or other forms of parental assistance (Kraft 1984). They are being pressed as issues in both hiring and retention. As institutions begin to compete for female talent in new ways, some institutions are also setting aside funds to offer attractive salary packages to women faculty (and dual-career couples) as well as to quietly correct past salary inequities. Some observers see a new appreciation for and willingness to pay for female faculty talent nationwide. If so, it should help to ameliorate the still pervasive salary gap of 15 to 25 percent.

The factor of gender added to the salary equity equation heightens the need for comprehensive adjustments and revisions in policy. The interrelatedness of salaries with other aspects of faculty life, such as promotion and tenure, precludes policies that focus on only one issue at a time. While affirmative action policies have initiated some progress on issues of sex equity, that progress has been slow and somewhat inadequate. No one denies that achieving equity costs money. Yet practices that are fair to women faculty, such as regular reviews of salary and rank, are also fair to men and need to be included as part of institutional policies of compensation and administration generally.

Race and Ethnicity

Given changing national demographics, salary and equity for faculty of color and other ethnic backgrounds should be an area of growing concern to researchers and policy makers. At present, however, little empirical research has actually been undertaken on these issues. Discussions have focused primarily on access to the academic marketplace and less on equitable treatment once faculty are hired (Smith and Witt 1990). Some evidence suggests that progress is being made, albeit slowly, in breaking down the barriers of access to academe for those who have traditionally been excluded (Harvey and Scott-Jones 1985; Justus, Freitag, and Parker 1987; Menges and Exum 1983; Newman 1979; Washington and Harvey 1989).

The few studies that have been conducted concerning minority faculty compensation found different results and different rationales for what they found. A study conducted in 1979 found that African-American faculty members received an average of $1,799 more than their white counterparts (H. Tuckman 1979), suggesting that a form of the supply-and-demand theory was operating. Affirmative action efforts initiated by the federal government had encouraged colleges and universities to hire more African-American faculty, but because the pool of faculty with the requisite credentials was limited, colleges and universities had to offer above-average salaries to them (Mackey-Smith 1984; Mooney 1989). Moreover, highly educated African-Americans come with higher opportunity costs because of increasing job opportunities in industry and government, which also drives up their salaries.

On the other hand, "the usual laws of supply and demand have not applied to African-American and Hispanics in higher education" (Washington and Harvey 1989, p. 26). Another study found that minority faculty were often paid approximately $1,000 less per year than white faculty (Exum 1983), attributing the lower salaries to the fact that African-Americans in particular have been more concentrated in lower ranks and in nontenured positions often connected with special programs for minority students. Recent work on the National Survey of Postsecondary Education Faculty found that minority faculty received approximately $1,000 less per year than majority faculty (Fairweather 1992). When disaggregated into more specific race and ethnic categories, however, the numbers of minority faculty are so small that more definite analyses are quite difficult.*

Interestingly, virtually all of the studies note that women faculty, minority or majority, tend to receive salaries below the average for minorities in general (Exum 1983; Fairweather 1992; H. Tuckman 1979). A particularly pernicious myth in higher education is that minority women are "prime hires" because they represent two "protected groups" (Washington and Harvey 1989). These findings have been confirmed, namely, that Hispanic and African-American women are at the bottom of the professorial ladder in numbers, rank, and salary (Wilson 1987).

Among minority males, only Asian men have had higher salaries than white men, largely because of the concentration of Asian males in engineering and the sciences (Exum 1983). African-American men tend to have among the lowest average salaries among minority men (Exum 1983).

Uniformly, the studies of minority faculty point to a discouraging tendency for lower salaries to be accompanied by heavier work loads, which include additional service and advising (Romero 1977). Thus, academic administrators should "ensure that salary equity exists and that multiple contributions of faculty from targeted populations to service, teaching, scholarship, mentoring, advising, and recruitment have been fully rewarded . . ." (Washington and Harvey 1989, p. 29).

Thus, the issues of equity for minority faculty begin with concerns about access but include issues of work load and the variety of services they render compared to what white colleagues are asked to do and rewarded for (Blackwell 1988; Elmore and Blackburn 1983; Laury 1988). Equity proceeds to overarching concerns for retaining the small number of minority faculty who are recruited to academe (Reed 1983).

Age

The Age Discrimination in Employment Act, passed in 1967 and amended in 1978 and 1986, applies to colleges and universities most directly with the lifting of limits on retirement age as of January 1994. While considerable research and rhetorical attention have been paid to the likely impact of a gray-

---

*James Fairweather 1992, personal communication.

ing professoriat and the uncapping of age limits on retirement, less attention has been paid to the issue of age discrimination in salaries. Our society has a general sense that "age has its privileges," and receiving greater compensation is presumed to be one of the privileges. People generally expect that they will be making more money and accruing more benefits as they age, but this situation is not always true.

In general, age and experience have important effects on the academic reward structure (Lawrence and Blackburn 1988). Rank structure correlates roughly with age and more deliberately with experience. Rank itself is correlated approximately with compensation levels, and "the relationship between age and salary peaks at age 49 and declines thereafter" (H. Tuckman 1979, p. 30). Basic salary peaks between the ages of 60 and 64 and declines thereafter (Fairweather 1992). This pattern of rising then declining salaries is consistent with age/earning profiles for most professional fields (Lawrence and Blackburn 1988).

Indeed, it is in this age/experience dimension of compensation that the professoriat shows its kinship with other professions. Professionals prefer to distinguish themselves from other types of workers based on their specialized training and expertise of a scientific or intellectual nature. Even within firms in the private sector, professionals often expect and receive separate status, compensation streams, and promotional opportunities (Milkovich and Newman 1990). Because the value of a professional lies in his or her special expertise, as that expertise becomes more dated, the corresponding yearly increments tend to decrease in size over time. For example, some engineering research and development firms calculate a "maturity track" that plots the empirical relationship between pay and years since a professional last earned a degree. Some universities use a similar calculation based on the year in which faculty members received their Ph.D. as a means of calculating both their starting salaries and the continuing relationship to their degree cohorts over time.

These calculations do not address the issue of productivity or experience but only years since birth or since receiving the Ph.D. While in general salary appears to tail off after about 50 years of age, it does necessarily reflect on a person's productivity or contributions. Insofar as compensation should be based on performance, broadly construed to also include experience, then a decline in salary need not occur in the later years of a faculty member's career. In fact, a college or university that exhibits the typical pattern of maturity might be subject to a question about whether the salaries of older faculty are being tied too closely to age rather than productivity (Kastenbaum and Schulte 1988).

If fact, some of the same compensation policies and institutional practices that work in favor of faculty early in their careers are less supportive of them as they mature. For instance, the traditional institutional rewards for productivity are very effective motivators for junior faculty (Tuckman 1987). Assistant professors are perhaps the most receptive because they recognize a direct relationship between their productivity and various rewards, such as salary increases, promotion, tenure, and enhanced career options. Senior faculty, who are established in their careers, do not necessarily respond to the same incentives as their junior colleagues— nor, in fact, do they receive the same return for their productivity as do junior faculty. Yet institutional polices and reward structures have changed very little to accommodate the needs of a growing senior faculty population.

The fact that raises are annuitized across a career buffers and slows some of the effect of aging. If a faculty member received high increases in the early or midcareer years, these dollars are added to the base salary that affects all subsequent annual raises. Thus, even if productivity declines in later years, the smaller merit raises in many cases are added to a larger base salary for a senior faculty member, softening the impact of declining performance for the senior faculty member even as it weakens the effect of higher performance of junior colleagues, comparatively speaking (Lawler 1990).

The rank structure, which serves as a basis for compensation policies at many institutions, provides few real opportunities to reward faculty significantly. After the first promotion to associate professor, only one further standard promotion is accompanied in most cases by a larger-than-average raise— the promotion to full professor. Beyond the point of tenure and status as full professor, the rank structure offers annual increases as virtually the only possible means for rewarding older, and usually more senior, faculty.

Salary compression
The issue that is more likely to spark anger from senior faculty is salary compression—the hiring of junior faculty at similar

or higher salaries than their more senior colleagues. Primarily as a result of market influences, entry-level salaries for assistant professors have been rising sharply in some fields, in turn narrowing the distribution of salaries across ranks. Because their entry-level (or base) salary is higher, the rate of increase in compensation for junior faculty is faster as well. The result is that, in some cases, salaries of junior professors quickly outpace those of their less mobile, senior colleagues (Annual Report 1988; Snyder, McLaughlin, and Montgomery 1992). Instead of being rewarded for their loyalty and long service, those faculty who build their careers at one institution could actually be penalized in terms of remuneration compared to their more junior colleagues.

Salary compression can also be found within ranks as a result of different rewards for productivity or cost opportunity factors that vary by discipline (H. Tuckman 1979). Sometimes referred to as "salary dispersion," the widening gap in salaries among disciplines is a cause of some concern in many institutions. Faculty of the same rank who work in different disciplines could be many thousands of dollars apart in salary.

A tendency for compression within ranks begins among junior faculty. New assistant professors are being recruited at salaries higher than those given to colleagues hired even one year earlier (Annual Report 1988). This trend, sometimes referred to as "negative tenure slope," is occurring at an increasing rate in many disciplines, including those often considered low-demand fields. Negative tenure slope is supposed to correct itself after the faculty member receives tenure.

The long-range effect on faculty remuneration from the structure of compensation and reliance on base salaries, however, should not be discounted as perpetuating salary concerns. Many studies show that age and rank still differentiate levels of salary for most faculty in most institutions. Yet the rising competition for a shrinking pool of junior faculty and growing dispersion of salaries among disciplines suggest these basic structural components of salary could be weakening.

Age and gender
Cases of sex discrimination can be entangled with issues of age because the disparity between men's and women's salaries is most pronounced in the senior ranks. Women receive a much smaller increase in salary from age 46 to age 50 than do men, and the difference continues to escalate thereafter

(Darland, Dawkins, and Lascich 1973; Fairweather 1992). Informal estimates suggest that academic women can fall behind male colleagues as much as $1,000 for every year of service after tenure (see also Fairweather 1992 and Smart 1991 for discussions of the power of gender effects in determining salary).

Age and legal issues

Class action suits based on age are relatively rare, and even individual suits are not common yet. But it is conceivable that as the professoriat generally continues to age, various compensation practices, such as hiring, raises, and overall compensation will be challenged more frequently if they show a pattern of discriminating against older faculty (Blum 1989; Mooney 1991).

The issue of age and equity also includes an embedded issue of productivity. Some faculty in their later years become less productive, out of date, or outmoded in their responses to students' interests. The promotion and tenure process works well in weeding out unproductive faculty early in their careers, but it also can protect them later. Institutional responses to the problems of low productivity and outmoded faculty expertise vary, even in light of tenure policies (Kastenbaum and Schulte 1988). But certain alternatives to termination and retirement can also revitalize senior faculty. While many reasons can exist for lower levels of productivity, lack of a positive reward structure is one that policy planners can address readily.

The challenge is to create compensation policies that respond to the needs and efforts of faculty throughout their careers (Schuster, Wheeler, and Associates 1990). Productive senior faculty should continue to feel their work is as valued as when they began their careers. Compensation policies should not present a forced choice between staying at one institution for an extended career and receiving sufficient remuneration. Programs need to be designed wisely and fairly so as to acknowledge the breadth of experience implicit in loyalty and longevity as well as productivity.

Equitable Pay

Based on the framework of laws and regulations noted earlier, it seems clear that academic compensation systems should incorporate a policy of equal pay for substantially equal work.

> *The challenge is to create compensation policies that respond to the needs and efforts of faculty throughout their careers.*

The determination of what constitutes substantially equal work, however, is extremely complicated. But the laws pertaining to equity in pay and the precedents established by the courts make it clear that any compensation policy must be based on the actual work performed and the basic job content, and must reflect the skill, effort, and responsibility required and the working conditions involved. It is legal to pay women and men differently who perform substantially equal work, provided the pay system is designed to recognize differences in performance, seniority, quantity and quality of results, or certain factors other than sex (such as market or merit) in a nondiscriminatory way. A one-time adjustment can correct past problems—apparent sex discrimination, for example—and those moneys can be applied to the affected group only. But if a new compensation system is implemented for all faculty, then that system must be applied equally to all (Milkovich and Newman 1990).

Knowledge of the laws pertaining to discrimination in pay should receive special attention by any administrators who deal with faculty salary and by faculty if they are involved in any process of awarding salary increases to colleagues. The laws are important because they regulate the administration and design of pay systems generally. Moreover, the consequences of being found guilty of discrimination in pay can have overwhelming financial and organizational implications. To ensure that every institution has well-defined and defensible practices of pay, continuous attention needs to be given to these laws. The way our society views equity in pay and discrimination in salary is changing considerably; action in the courts and on campuses across the nation is structuring present and future policies and practices of compensation.

Three basic qualities of a sound pay system are embedded in the laws and the court cases: pay practices must be work related, they must be related to the mission of the organization, and they must include an appeals process for employees who disagree with the results (Milkovich and Newman 1990, p. 489). Pay practices that discriminate against faculty members simply on the basis of their sex, race, age, or other characteristics, when it can be shown that such factors are not truly work related or concerned with the mission of the college or university, are subject to challenge. Moreover, faculty members, like all other employees, should have the right to know on what basis they are being paid, on what basis raises or bonuses are being provided, and how they as individuals are being evaluated with respect to their unit's pay practices.

In many colleges and universities, a strong tradition of shared governance means that faculty are involved in the evaluation and awarding of pay increases. Such faculty in particular should be apprised of all laws and policies that might pertain to their activities with respect to pay. On other campuses, faculty salaries are a closely guarded secret of administration. In those situations, faculty members still have a right to know the grounds for their salaries and should definitely have the clear right of appeal. Moreover, the laws extend many of these protections to individuals as members of affected groups. Implicit, therefore, in equitable compensation practices is an information system that permits examination of those pay practices as they pertain to individuals and to such groups as women, minorities, and senior faculty.

Summary

In the steady-state 1970s, when few faculty were hired, most issues of faculty compensation concerned annual increases, promotions, or compensation for extra activities. As hiring pressures have built in the 1980s and into the 1990s, however, so have the demands for more sophisticated policies and procedures on salary. The influence of a variety of new factors, such as gender, race, and age, as well as more traditional market factors and issues related to the disciplinary nature of higher education, contain a host of issues regarding equity for salary administrators. Overarching all of them is the need to reconcile such factors with institutional mission and academic values so as not to perpetuate the negative effects of a multitiered, multidimensional system of faculty remuneration.

BUILDING EFFECTIVE COMPENSATION SYSTEMS

Academic compensation is a mosaic of policies, procedures, precedents, laws, norms, and values. It has evolved piecemeal by responding to changing markets, individual expectations and behaviors, and institutional circumstances. Some view this highly complex and diverse system as the artifact of a struggle between, on the one hand, faculty who seek to optimize their own personal and professional situation and, on the other hand, increasingly bureaucratic organizations that seek to maximize their command and control over key human resources. In fact, compensation systems should seek to achieve a reasonable balance between the faculty's personal and professional needs and a college's or university's mission, goals, and resources.

From the faculty's perspective, compensation by itself is not a precise indicator of financial well-being. Many other elements enter into determining how the professoriat is faring compared to other professions and compared to other points in time. Such things as cost of living in general and in specific locations, personal life-styles, institutional fiscal health, and several other factors need to be examined to establish the faculty's overall financial well-being. Yet compensation is central and deserves sustained and careful attention from both faculty and administrators.

From the institution's perspective, recent studies of the professoriat point to the need for better management of human resources (Bowen and Schuster 1986; Burke 1987). A variety of circumstances are changing the composition and values of the professoriat, including altered views toward career, the quality of academic life, and changing family structures—all of which affect systems of compensation. Competition among institutions and between the academic, private, and government sectors for Ph.D.s is intensifying. Advances in information technology and the development of knowledge are creating expanding networks for faculty to work in national and global arenas. These and other changes will affect compensation for faculty.

Compensation also is part of a social system on any campus in which salary is important less for what it will buy and more for what it symbolizes about what that institution and the faculty within it value (McKeachie 1979). For some faculty, the nonmonetary conditions of employment—good facilities and libraries and stimulating students and colleagues—are far more important to their productivity, satisfaction, and career stability than their pay. For others, however, direct monetary rewards are important both for their real and symbolic value. And some faculty work assiduously to command high salaries and other financial rewards.

Monetary rewards can vary dramatically by academic specialty, type of institution, degree of productivity, and personal characteristics like gender, race, and age. These variations are related not only to specific institutional aims and objectives, but also to the culture and values of the college or university where they are found. Moreover, certain variations are patterned, thereby providing broad contours to the profession as a whole. For example, the finding that research publication is more rewarded than is teaching or other faculty activities at virtually all types of institutions for all types of faculty has been repeated in study after study since the early 1970s. Or consider the general finding concerning gender that women are paid less than men at all ranks, in most disciplines, and in most types of institutions. Another universal contour is the faculty member's field or discipline. "Direct monetary rewards differ, in some cases dramatically, by academic field" (H. Tuckman 1979, p. 172). These patterned variations in compensation are powerful, defining dimensions of the conditions of the professoriat.

From the point of view of the college or university as an employing organization, a set of policy dimensions form the foundation of any compensation system: internal consistency, external competition, individual contributions, and administration of compensation systems (Milkovich and Newman 1990).

Internal Consistency

One of the most difficult challenges for administrators of pay systems in colleges and universities is to establish and maintain a system that is internally consistent. In fact, this principle is both controversial and problematic in many institutions. It is controversial because many faculty and administrators believe that competition should be the main basis for setting compensation—namely, what salary will attract and retain the most talented individuals. Consistency is problematic because the custom of individualized negotiations combined with the relative autonomy of many departments creates difficult-to-control variations within an institution, leading both to salary dispersion and salary compression and sometimes to claims of inequity.

Even within a given department, it is difficult to hold to a principle of consistency because individuals possess different backgrounds and skills and bring different concerns to the negotiations. It is often difficult to say what an associate professor does as a generality within a department, much less on an institutionwide basis. Thus, when provosts or deans attempt to articulate a policy based on consistency—one that states that men and women who are hired at the same rank in the same or related disciplines at the same time should receive identical starting salaries, for example—the administrators are likely to face resistance from both department chairs and job candidates, each of whom may prefer to establish salaries based on individual negotiations. Establishing salary ranges can be equally problematic given these other pressures.

In industry, strategies for job assessment are built around the principle of internal consistency. In academe, however, while support and clerical staff might be subject to job assessment, few faculty positions are treated in this manner. The closest approximation comes in collective bargaining agreements, where student contact hours, course loads, and other duties can be specified. Some small colleges might also implement more uniform salary ranges across the campus and constrain what can be negotiated with new hires.

External Competition

External competition shapes both policy and practice in higher education institutions—but not always in clearly understood ways. Positioning an institution's compensation system relative to other competitors is not easy given the many variables that need to be taken into account, including discipline, rank, individual credentials, and the type of competitors (peer institutions, business, or government).

From the department's perspective, each unit usually attempts to optimize its talent as well as its resources relative to other units on the campus as well as peer departments elsewhere. Thus, a given department will seek to hire the most talented individuals it can and will often side with the job candidate in seeking the best salary terms that it can on behalf of the person, in part because the salary and other resources will come to the department and add to its base. For this and other reasons, internal competition for resources and external competition for talented individuals, in combination, tend to boost rather than deflate salaries.

The highest reaches of the institution should show a concern for linking salary decisions with the overall strategic and operating objectives of the college or university. That is, in hiring faculty for a given unit, a key administrator associated with the decision should ask, How much do we want to spend and need to spend to get an individual of this quality for this unit? Such an assessment should be tied to a larger analysis of the quality of the unit compared to others within the institution and compared to others within the same general field at other institutions. Naturally, it costs more to raise the quality of a large unit because more individuals of higher quality have to be hired. It also costs more to raise the quality of a high-paying field. Investments on a large scale, involving the commitment of institutional resources for more than one or two positions within a given unit, require especially careful consideration and planning. Annual salary adjustments are constrained by projected institutional revenue. Long-term salary commitments based on overall hiring plans need to be connected within the campus to a clear sense of mission and objectives.

In addition to such unit-based investments to rebuild a given department or to add a particular discipline, strategic initiatives might be established through affirmative action to encourage hiring women and minorities. Special funds could be established to hire such individuals. Often the field of the scholar is not specified, but units can request additional funds or, in some cases, additional faculty lines. In such cases, often a persuasive combination consists of a willingness to invest in a particular unit and a desire to increase the number of talented minority and female faculty.

In times of severe fiscal challenge, the trade-offs between faculty salaries and other expenditures need to be calculated carefully. Just as across-the-board raises tend to spread money evenly and also to preserve the status quo, so across-the-board cuts to departments share the pain but also do little to master the direction of change. Across-the-board cuts and/or the withholding of salary raises can levy unintended collateral damage to faculty because of current circumstances in some departments. Such actions can foster vulnerability to raids from other institutions, unplanned and undesired departures of key faculty into early retirement or to other jobs, job refusals from faculty recruits, and declines in the number of graduate student applications.

Several agencies and institutions compile salary information on an annual basis by field, rank, and sometimes gender and race to assist campus administrators to place their salary levels in a comparative perspective. The information provided by the AAUP, Oklahoma State University, the U.S. Department of Education, and several consortia of institutions is useful to colleges and universities seeking to position themselves wisely and efficiently in the marketplace. Such information is also helpful to individuals but only in a general way, because circumstances of a particular job offer or continuing faculty position are so individualized.

Individual Contributions

A third policy arena concerns individual contributions. What is the institution's relative emphasis on performance compared to such other considerations as seniority, years of experience, or other factors for people holding the same job? Merit is a central value of the academic profession, but it is a complex one. Many factors must be considered in trying to link pay to performance in academe. In general, faculty are skeptical of evaluation processes and rewards that do not link pay to performance. But the processes by which this link can be accomplished are not well articulated in many institutions. Faculty evaluation systems, for example, are quite problematic. How well do we evaluate the work faculty do in teaching, research, and service? Most would claim we do a fairly good job in the area of research, at least compared to the other two areas, which is why, some argue, research activity is better rewarded. But overall, our systems of evaluation are not well developed or fully engaged. Moreover, faculty evaluation tends to function best in the early stages of a faculty member's career, which could be why rewards are also greatest at the lowest ranks. At the rank of associate and full professor, the rewards are not as consistent, as frequent, or as large, relatively speaking, as they are in the lower ranks. Very senior faculty are perhaps the most neglected group of all when considering merit or evaluation systems generally.

Although many institutions do have merit systems, these systems are complicated to administer fairly and consistently. It is "impossible to have a merit pay system that does an effective job of both motivating performance and retaining the best performers. One of these two highly desirable objectives has to be sacrificed because of the annuity feature of merit pay" (Lawler 1990, p. 75)—a reference to the fact that early good performers accumulate the advantage of being rewarded for that performance quite apart from their later performance. Thus, rewarding the truly best performers the most in any given round of merit raises is virtually impossible because of the annuity factor others bring into the process of setting rewards.

We do not understand a great deal about the motivational power of compensation on faculty behavior. We do not know to what extent changes in salary, raises based on merit, or other aspects of salary actually motivate faculty to change their behavior. For example, what is the effect of compensation on the decision to change jobs? Do faculty decide to leave their current institution for another because of their pay? What amount of money if any will induce a faculty member to change the allocation of time? This problem confronts many institutions that wish to motivate faculty to spend more time and energy in teaching compared to publishing. Is money the best incentive to get them to do so? If so, how much money and in what form—direct salary or benefit or a combination?

Even the notion that salary is an incentive for future performance as well as a reward for past performance is not well understood. For some people, pay is a way to help them assess and rate their success compared to others; pay serves, both directly and indirectly, as a symbol of success. For others, pay is important because it is connected to other things they value, such as prestige or status. "People will always value $2,000 more than $1,000, but perhaps not twice as much" (Lawler 1990, p. 16). For example, it is not uncommon for senior faculty to offer to forgo an annual raise in favor of using the money to assist graduate students or to purchase needed supplies and services. In short, salary might be important to faculty but not solely as dollars in their pockets, and not compared to other things they might value as much or more.

Administration of Compensation Systems

The final aspect of an effective compensation system is its administration. Compensation should be linked to the overall mission and goals of the college or university, and it can serve as a vital instrument in accomplishing both strategic and regular operating objectives. The compensation system must be linked to the regular planning, budgeting, and evaluation systems for faculty as well. An unconstrained compensation system can wreak havoc with any college or university's overall effectiveness. Several factors must be kept in mind in administering compensation: efficiency, procedural equity, communication, and evaluation.

Efficiency

With respect to efficiency, a key cost in administration is how much time is involved and how complicated the various salary and compensation processes being used are. On many campuses, both faculty and administrators have a hand in these processes. Faculty committees often are involved in determining merit raises, in identifying if not selecting likely faculty recruits, in negotiating salary itself, and sometimes in recommending various salary policies and procedures for their departments and for the institution as a whole. Any and all of these operations can be complicated and time-consuming. The direct administration of salary by staff as well as by department heads, deans, and other administrators can consume large amounts of time also.

Training to carry out these tasks is often spotty or nonexistent. In few institutions are department heads provided with training about the theory and practice of faculty compensation. Most department chairs must learn the ropes about compensation on the job and through informal discussions with faculty and other administrators. In some cases, formal written procedures are available, but in many cases they are not. In short, many administrators are not prepared for the intricacies involved in using compensation to hire, retain, and motivate faculty, including the time they can spend in hearing grievances emanating from these processes.

Procedural equity

Procedural equity involves the process used to establish and implement salary decisions. For many faculty, these processes are just as important as the outcome. In fact, faculty members' perceptions about the fairness of the process will directly affect their acceptance of the results.

According to compensation experts, pay procedures are more likely to be perceived as fair if those affected are repre-

In few institutions are department heads provided with training about the theory and practice of faculty compensation.

sented or participate in the process, if the data used are known in advance and accurate, if the procedures are applied consistently, and if the possibility for appeals exists (Lawler 1990; Milkovich and Newman 1990). Many institutions have been careful to establish procedural equity with respect to promotion and tenure but have been less consistent in terms of compensation processes. While some faculty are content to let administrators decide, others would subscribe to the principles enunciated earlier. Undercutting the notion of procedural equity in determining pay might be the custom of individual negotiation. Certainly academe is rife with undercurrents of complaint about faculty salaries, some of which might be alleviated if these principles were followed.

Faculty members' satisfaction or dissatisfaction with salary is based on comparisons with colleagues' salaries on campus and outside. Most faculty compare notes based on what they know about their colleagues' qualifications for their jobs, the kind of work being done, and the quality and value of the work performed compared to their own. Within the context of their own discipline and department, faculty then gain an impression of what are the likely salary returns for investing time and effort in particular kinds of work. These impressions might or might not be accurate unless actual salary criteria are both made public and adhered to in determining salary.

"The better, clearer, and more equally applied the procedures that institutions have, the more likely that their employment relationship with faculty will go unchallenged, or if challenged, will be left unscathed" (Lee and Olswang 1985, p. 243). Clearly written and concise procedures based on objective evidence and reviewed regularly accomplish two equally important objectives. They provide the documentation individual faculty need to judge their performance, and they provide the documentation administrators need to make decisions about salary and to defend them against allegations of unfairness or discrimination.

Communication
The importance of clear and accurate communication about salary procedures, criteria, and results cannot be overstated. Faculty do base their behavior on their perceptions of the nature of the rewards and incentives in their institution. Such behavior might range from how to spend their time daily to whether or not to look for a different job. While an individ-

ual's perceptions are indeed personal, many institutions can do far more to communicate about their compensation system to faculty. The importance of perceptions to faculty's subsequent beliefs and behaviors should not be left to chance. "If fair procedures and structures have been designed, part of administering them involves insuring [that] employees believe they are fair" (Milkovich and Newman 1990, p. 44).

The benefits program and related costs require careful monitoring and regular communication to faculty. The mix of costs to the institution and to the faculty member might change as the result of introducing cafeteria-style benefits plans or as the result of reduced revenues to pay for selected benefits within the institutional budget. Separate elements of the benefits program require monitoring and analysis, such as health insurance, social security, and, especially, retirement programs. Retirement costs can be the single largest element in the benefits program (Waggamon 1983). Retirement is a particularly volatile issue and deserves special attention.

A particular challenge for institutions at present is to maintain quality and productivity in the face of retrenchment and declining revenues. Appropriate policies and procedures for compensation must be devised that preserve existing quality but also allow the institution to adapt to changing circumstances and that encourage faculty to enhance their development along institutionally congruent lines. One of the chief tools for meeting these challenges is an information system that clearly communicates the policies and procedures involved in faculty compensation, those with authority and responsibility for its administration, the performance criteria used to increase salaries, and how faculty can participate in the ongoing development of the system itself.

Evaluation
Dissatisfaction with salary is common among faculty. It is a view that is perhaps rightly held when the professoriat is compared to other professions. But it is so pervasive among faculty that a more penetrating concern should be which faculty members are most dissatisfied and whether they are more dissatisfied than faculty at other institutions. Regrettably, many institutions cannot answer these two basic questions.

Salary costs constitute a large share of an institution's budget. Clearly, what is occurring in salaries and benefits compared to other areas of the budget needs to be monitored.

But beyond that, it is vital to know how effective the compensation system is, requiring an information system that can generate data on such things as how competitive salaries are for the type of institution and the quality of faculty present or desired. Are salaries losing ground in the face of declining institutional revenues, rising inflation, or institutional competitors? Does the institution have problems in the area of salary compression or dispersion, and is it affecting faculty morale? Is the rate of faculty turnover changing, and do exit interviews indicate that salary is one of the causes? How are departments doing in hiring top candidates? Are salaries fair by rank, experience, gender, race, and discipline? Does the institution show evidence of discriminating on the basis of age? Where do part-time faculty stand? Are their salaries fair and competitive?

Additional thought needs to be given to the cost–quality–productivity equation. Given reduced resources at many institutions, every dollar spent on faculty has increasing value. But it is not always clear that simply increasing salaries will result in increased quality or performance. Should an institution invest in new faculty, who are becoming increasingly expensive to hire, or in continuing faculty, who, while costly, might provide or be encouraged to provide contributions needed in areas junior faculty are unlikely to be interested in, such as student advising and other services? Unless a college or university knows how much it costs to hire a junior faculty member, including salary, recruitment, and start-up costs, compared to costs associated with sabbaticals and other developmental activities for senior faculty, decision makers do not have the complete information they need to make wise, long-term decisions (Ehrenberg, Kasper, and Rees 1991).

To consider salary raises and other pieces of compensation as incentives for increased or higher-quality faculty performance requires that existing incentives be evaluated to see what types of practices and behaviors they support (Levin 1991). The findings should be compared with the goals and objectives of the college or university and possibly a new system of both departmental and individual rewards and incentives established that encourages faculty and departmental activities more in line with the desired goals. Recently, several writers have proposed the idea of shared savings and carry-over funding for departments to encourage innovation and provide rewards for improved performance or efficiency by faculty on a departmental basis rather than an individual one (Chait 1988; Langenburg 1992; Levin 1991).

Problems also arise in providing adequate performance measures to serve as incentives. For example, for measures of faculty performance to be effective in encouraging faculty to spend time and energy in improvement, the measures must be seen as both credible and also susceptible to being influenced by the faculty members themselves. The powerful part about many measures of research productivity is that they are seen as both credible and able to be influenced. For example, peer review of publications and the incremental rewards attached to quantity of publications appear to be powerful incentives that encourage faculty to engage in research. In contrast, many measures of teaching are not subject to serious peer review, and some, like student evaluations, appear only indirectly related to how much effort a faculty member puts into teaching.

Efficiency, procedural equity, communication, and evaluation are indispensable elements of an effective compensation system. When these elements undergird the administration of compensation, the system will be more credible and have greater integrity. Individual situations can be attended to while keeping the institution's overall objectives in focus.

Summary

The purpose of this report has been to present a comprehensive view of faculty compensation. The national perspective on faculty needs and concerns underscores the importance of sound compensation policies. The environment for hiring and retaining talented individuals within the academic profession is growing more turbulent. The necessity for fiscal restraint has not lessened; rather, the multiple demands on financial resources continue to grow. Not least among these concerns are faculty salaries, annual increases, and fringe benefits.

Examining a series of dominant issues like the structure and uses of compensation, the impact of the academic labor market, and multiple forms of equity had as its aim to show both the complexity and the dynamism of faculty compensation. All of these issues form a matrix, the two principle axes being the institution and its mission and objectives, and the faculty and their interests and aspirations. The point is that when an issue is addressed from one perspective of the matrix, the opposite side is affected. For example, if senior faculty postpone retirement, they continue to command higher salaries, which in turn affects which positions are available to junior faculty and what salaries can be offered them.

Policies and practices affecting compensation form an intangible but significant web of values and actions. Seldom are they examined comprehensively institutionally or nationally. Rather, the day-to-day routine and the exigencies of annual salary processes tend to determine actions for the future— a shortsighted, even perilous, view, given the current national environment. In fact, institutional policies and practices do not operate in a vacuum. Numerous factors, including student enrollments, federal and state aid, and tax policy, significantly affect faculty, their work, and their pay.

While only local administrators and faculty leaders are in the best positions to weigh the various factors that must make up a college or university's compensation policy, this report places these local situations in a broader context. Discussions must necessarily shift between these two perspectives. Nevertheless, certain principles emerge. First is the need for balance. Overemphasis on the interests or concerns of one type of faculty or one area of policy is likely to jeopardize other, equally important concerns. For example, if an institution with limited resources chooses to pursue high-priced faculty at all costs, it is likely to create new problems, such as salary compression, and threaten other aspects of its compensation system, not least faculty morale. Similarly, if an institution tries to treat all faculty the same in its compensation plan, eventually the most productive, the most senior, or other valued but somewhat special individuals or groups of faculty are likely to become disaffected. These scenarios do not argue for a policy of willy-nilly consideration; rather, they call for more complex and careful consideration of what policies are in place, their effects (both intended and unintended), and how well they correspond with and support the values and objectives the institution wishes to embody in its faculty. Keeping these concerns in balance is imperative at least in the long run.

A second principle is flexibility. An institution whose resources for compensation are totally committed to meeting today's payroll will have little prospect of meeting tomorrow's new demands. Higher education in the United States is facing a major change in its faculty as the G.I. generation of scholars exits the academic stage. Who will replace them? What disciplines and skills will these new scholars possess? And how will they fit with institutional needs and values? Until these changes are well under way, the environment will be extremely challenging. Institutions must deal with large numbers of retiring faculty and recruit new ones at the same time. A flexible response is vital for preserving a clear sense of who and what the faculty are.

A third principle is fairness, broadly defined. Few issues are as difficult to deal with as equity. Equity wears many faces. In some respects, the least equitable approach is to try to treat all faculty alike. At the same time, satisfactory remedies for inequities are not always the same; that is, more money is not invariably the best answer. Other forms of reward and recognition might be just as important as dollars. In other circumstances, more money is the answer, and so it must be found within the institution's budget. Thoughtful and informed dialogue between administrators and faculty and with other parties in the policy arena must be continuous. Thus, administrators must be willing to engage in open discussion of budget matters and evaluation criteria, and faculty must strive for an institutionwide perspective. All must work toward clear polices and equitable procedures for making decisions about compensation.

Dealing with compensation in the coming years will be much like swimming. No one who is involved can avoid getting wet. The goal ought not to be mere survival; rather, the goal must be a sense of shared values and shared accomplishment. At stake is not merely tomorrow's payroll but tomorrow itself.

REFERENCES

The Educational Resources Information Center (ERIC) Clearinghouse
on Higher Education abstracts and indexes the current literature on
higher education for inclusion in ERIC's data base and announce-
ment in ERIC's monthly bibliographic journal, *Resources in Education* (RIE). Most of these publications are available through the
ERIC Document Reproduction Service (EDRS). For publications cited
in this bibliography that are available from EDRS, ordering number
and price code are included. Readers who wish to order a publication should write to the ERIC Document Reproduction Service,
7420 Fullerton Rd., Suite 110, Springfield, VA 22153-2852. (Phone
orders with VISA or MasterCard are taken at 800-443-ERIC or
703-440-1400.) When ordering, please specify the document (ED)
number. Documents are available as noted in microfiche (MF) and
paper copy (PC). If you have the price code ready when you call
EDRS, an exact price can be quoted. The last page of the latest issue
of *Resources in Education* also has the current cost, listed by code.

Amey, Marilyn J. 1991. "Faculty Issues for the 1990s." Report prepared
for the executive vice chancellor and the campus planning and
advisory committee. Lawrence: Univ. of Kansas.
————. 1992. "Faculty Recruitment, Tenure, and Promotion." In *The
Encyclopedia for Higher Education,* edited by Burton R. Clark and
Guy R. Neave. Oxford: Pergamon Press.
Anderson, Richard E., and Joel W. Meyerson. 1987. "Editor's Notes."
In *Financing Higher Education: Strategies after Tax Reform,* edited
by Richard E. Anderson and Joel W. Meyerson. New Directions
for Higher Education No. 58. San Francisco: Jossey-Bass.
Annual Report. 1988. "Mastering the Academic Marketplace." Annual
Report on the Economic Status of the Profession, 1987–88. *Academe* 74(2): 3–7.
————. 1990. "Some Dynamic Aspects of Academic Careers: The
Urgent Need to Match Aspirations with Compensation." Annual
Report on the Economic Status of the Profession, 1989–90. *Academe* 76(2): 3–10.
————. 1991. "The Future of Academic Salaries: Will the 1990s Be
a Bust like the 1970s or a Boom like the 1980s?" Annual Report
on the Economic Status of the Profession, 1990–91. *Academe*
77(2): 3–10.
Austin, Ann E. 1987. "Comparison of Faculty Perceptions of the Workplace at Low and High Morale Colleges." *The Future of the Academic Workplace in Liberal Arts Colleges.* Washington D.C.: Council
of Independent Colleges.
Backhus, DeWayne. 1992. "Faculty Workload as a Function of Career
Stage at Four-year Public Comprehensive Colleges or Universities."
Doctoral dissertation, Univ. of Kansas.
Baker, George P., Michael C. Jensen, and Kevin J. Murphy. 1988.

"Compensation and Incentives: Practice versus Theory." *Journal of Finance* 43(3): 593–616.

Baker, H. Kent. 1984. "The Impact of Collective Bargaining on Faculty Compensation in Community Colleges." *Community/Junior College Quarterly of Research and Practice* 8(1–4): 193–203.

Baldwin, Roger G. 1979. "The Faculty Career Process: Continuity and Change. A Study of College Professors at Five Stages of the Academic Year." Doctoral dissertation, Univ. of Michigan.

―――. 1990. "Faculty Career Stages and Implications for Professional Development." In *Enhancing Faculty Careers: Strategies for Development and Renewal,* edited by Jack H. Schuster, Daniel W. Wheeler, and Associates. San Francisco: Jossey-Bass.

Baldwin, Roger G., and Robert T. Blackburn. 1981. "The Academic Career as a Developmental Process: Implications for Higher Education." *Journal of Higher Education* 52(6): 598–614.

Baldwin, Roger G., and Marsha V. Krotseng. 1985. "Incentives in the Academic: Issues and Options." In *Incentives for Faculty Vitality,* edited by Roger G. Baldwin. New Directions for Higher Education No. 51. San Francisco: Jossey-Bass.

Barbezat, Debra A. 1987a. "The Effect of Collective Bargaining on Academic Salaries." Unpublished paper. Amherst, Mass.: Amherst College.

―――. 1987b. "Salary Differentials or Sex Discrimination? Evidence from the Academic Labor Market." *Population Research Policy Review* 6(1): 69–84.

―――. 1988. "Gender Differences in the Academic Reward System." In *Academic Labor Markets and Careers in American Higher Education,* edited by David W. Breneman and Ted Il Koo Youn. New York: Falmer Press.

Barnett, Harold, Jerry L. Cohen, Perry Jeffries, and William Rosen. 1988. "Coping with Merit Pay." *Academe* 74(6): 19–22.

Bassis, Michael S., and Alan E. Guskin. 1986. "Building Quality: Research and the Regional Institution." *Change* 18(4): 57–60.

Bayer, Alan E., and Helen S. Astin. 1975. "Gender Differentials in the Academic Reward Structure." *Science* 188: 796–802.

Becker, Gary S. 1975. *Human Capital: A Theoretical and Empirical Analysis, with Special Reference to Education.* 2d ed. New York: Columbia Univ. Press.

Becker, William E., Jr. 1985. "Maintaining Faculty Vitality through Collective Bargaining." In *Faculty Vitality and Institutional Productivity: Critical Perspectives for Higher Education,* edited by Shirley M. Clark and Darrell R. Lewis. New York: Teachers College Press.

Begin, J.P. 1979. "Faculty Bargaining and Faculty Reward Systems." In *Academic Rewards in Higher Education,* edited by Darrell R. Lewis and William E. Becker, Jr. Cambridge, Mass.: Ballenger

Publishing Co.

Bellah, Robert N., Richard Madsen, William M. Sullivan, and Others. 1985. *Habits of the Heart: Individualism and Commitment in American Life*. Berkeley: Univ. of California Press.

Bergmann, Barbara R. 1985. "Comparable Worth for Professors." *Academe* 71(4): 8–10.

Birnbaum, Michael. 1979. "Procedures for the Detection and Correction of Salary Equalities." In *Salary Equity*, edited by Thomas R. Pezzullo and Barbara E. Brittingham. Lexington, Mass.: Lexington Books.

Bishop, John. 1987. "The Recognition and Reward of Employee Performance." *Journal of Labor Economics* 5: S36–S56.

Blackburn, Robert T. 1985. "Faculty Career Development: Theory and Practice." In *Faculty Vitality and Institutional Productivity: Critical Perspectives for Higher Education*, edited by Shirley M. Clark and Darrell R. Lewis. New York: Teachers College Press.

Blackburn, Robert T., and Betty J. Holbert. 1987. "The Careers of Women in Academia." In *The Trapped Women: Catch-22 in Deviance and Control*, edited by Josephine Figueira-McDonough and Rosemary C. Sarri. Newbury Park, Calif.: Sage.

Blackwell, J.E. 1988. "Faculty Issues: The Impact on Minorities." *Review of Higher Education* 11(8): 417–34.

Blum, Debra E. 3 May 1989. "Bargaining Is Stalled among Professors, Study Center Shows." *Chronicle of Higher Education* 35(34): 15.

Bowen, Howard R. 1979. *Academic Compensation: Are Faculty and Staff in American Higher Education Adequately Paid?* New York: Teachers Insurance and Equity Association, College Retirement Equities Fund.

Bowen, Howard R., and Jack H. Schuster. 1986. *American Professors: A National Resource Imperiled*. New York: Oxford Univ. Press.

Bowen, William G., and Julie Ann Sosa. 1989. *Prospects for Faculty in the Arts and Sciences: A Study of Factors Affecting Demand and Supply, 1987–2012*. Princeton, N.J.: Princeton Univ. Press.

Boyer, Carol M., and Darrell R. Lewis. 1984. "Faculty Consulting: Responsibility or Promiscuity?" *Journal of Higher Education* 55(5): 637–59.

————. 1985. *And on the Seventh Day: Faculty Consulting and Supplemental Income*. ASHE-ERIC Higher Education Report No.3. Washington, D.C.: Association for the Study of Higher Education. ED 262 743. 89 pp. MF–01; PC–04.

Boyer, Ernest L. 1990. *Scholarship Reconsidered: Priorities of the Professoriate*. Princeton, N.J.: Carnegie Foundation for the Advancement of Teaching. ED 326 149. 151 pp. MF–01; PC not available EDRS.

Braskamp, Larry A., John A. Muffo, and Ira W. Langston III. 1978. "Determining Salary Equity: Policies, Procedures, and Problems."

Journal of Higher Education 49(30): 231–46.

Braudy, Leo. 1988. "Individual Careers versus Professional Lockstep: Problems of the Faculty Reward System." *ADE Bulletin* 89: 15–19.

Breneman, David W., and Ted Il Koo Youn, eds. 1988. *Academic Labor Markets and Careers in American Higher Education.* New York: Falmer Press.

Brown, David G. 1965. *The Market for College Teachers: An Economic Analysis of Career Patterns among Southeastern Social Scientists.* Durham, N.C.: Univ. of North Carolina Press.

Buchele, Robert, and Mark Aldrich. 1985. "How Much Difference Would Comparable Worth Make?" *Industrial Relations* 24(2): 222–33.

Burgan, Mary A. 1988. "The Faculty and the Superstar Syndrome." *Academe* 74(3): 10–14.

Burgess, Sylvia M. June/July 1985. "Cafeteria Plans and Alternative Methods for Providing Taxable Benefits to Employees." *Compensation Planning Journal:* 166–92.

Burke, Dolores L. 1987. "The Academic Marketplace in the 1980s: Appointment and Termination of Assistant Professors." *Review of Higher Education* 10(3): 199–214.

———. 1988. "An Overview of the 1987 ASHE Dissertation 'Change in the Academic Marketplace: Faculty Mobility in the 1980s.'" *Review of Higher Education* 11(3): 311–17.

Calais, Mary Jane. 1991. "The Future of Fringe Benefits: An Interview." *Academe* 77(3): 22.

Cameron, Kim. 1984. "Organizational Adaption and Higher Education." *Journal of Higher Education* 55(2): 122–44.

Camp, Robert C., Manton C. Gibbs, Jr., and Robert J. Masters II. 1988. "The Finite Increment Faculty Merit Pay Allocation Model." *Journal of Higher Education* 59(6): 652–67.

Carnegie Foundation for the Advancement of Teaching. 1990. "Are Liberal Arts Colleges Really Different?" *Change* 22(2): 41–44.

Centra, John A. 1985. "Maintaining Faculty Vitality through Faculty Development." In *Faculty Vitality and Institutional Productivity: Critical Perspectives for Higher Education,* edited by Shirley M. Clark and Darrell R. Lewis. New York: Teachers College Press.

Chaffee, Ellen Earle. 1985. "Three Models of Strategy." *Academy of Management Review* 10(1): 89–98.

Chait, Richard. 1988. "Providing Group Rewards for Group Performance." *Academe* 74(6): 23–24.

Chronister, Jay L. 1990. "Designing Options for Early Retirement." In *Enhancing Faculty Careers: Strategies for Development and Renewal,* edited by Jack H. Schuster, Daniel W. Wheeler, and Associates. San Francisco: Jossey-Bass.

Clark, Burton R. 1988. "The Absorbing Errand." *AAHE Bulletin* 40(7): 8–11.

Clark, Henry B., and Kristine E. Dillon. 1982. "The Ethics of the Academic Profession." In *Dollars and Scholars: An Inquiry into the Impact of Faculty Income upon the Function and Future of the Academy,* edited by Robert H. Linnell. Los Angeles: Univ. of Southern California Press.

Clark, Shirley M., and Mary Corcoran. 1986. "Perspectives on the Professional Socialization of Women Faculty: A Case of Accumulative Disadvantage?" *Journal of Higher Education* 57(1): 20–43.

Clark, Shirley M., and Darrell R. Lewis. 1985. "Implications for Institutional Response." In *Faculty Vitality and Institutional Productivity: Critical Perspectives for Higher Education,* edited by Shirley M. Clark and Darrell R. Lewis. New York: Teachers College Press.

Cole, Jonathan R. 1979. *Fair Science: Women in the Scientific Community.* New York: Free Press.

Creswell, John W. 1985. *Faculty Research Performance: Lessons from the Sciences and Social Sciences.* ASHE-ERIC Higher Education Report No. 4. Washington, D.C.: Association for the Study of Higher Education. ED 267 677. 88 pp. MF–01; PC–04.

Cross, K. Patricia. 1984. *Adults as Learners.* San Francisco: Jossey-Bass.

———. 1986. "Taking Teaching Seriously." Paper presented at an annual meeting of the American Association for Higher Education, Washington, D.C. ED 284 486. 6 pp. MF–01; PC–01.

Darland, M.G., S.M. Dawkins, and J.L. Lascich. 1973. "Application of Multivariate Regression to Studies of Salary Differences between Men and Women Faculty." Proceedings in the Social Statistics Section. Washington, D.C.: American Statistical Association.

D'Emilio, John. 1990. "The Campus Environment for Gay and Lesbian Life." *Academe* 76(1): 16–19.

Dickens, William T., and Kevin Lang. 1985. "A Test of Dual Market Theory." *American Economic Review* 75: 792–805.

Dillon, Kristine E., and Karen L. Bane. 1980. "Consulting and Conflict of Interest." *Educational Record* 6(2): 52–72.

Dillon, Kristine E., and Robert H. Linnell. 1980. "How and for What Are Professors Paid?" *Phi Kappa Phi Journal* 60(2): 21–23.

Dooris, Michael J., and Gregory G. Lozier. 1989. "Responding to the Challenge." In *Managing Faculty Resources,* edited by Gregory G. Lozier and Michael J. Dooris. New Directions for Institutional Research No. 63. San Francisco: Jossey-Bass.

Ehrenberg, Ronald, Hirschel Kasper, and Daniel Rees. 1991. "Faculty Turnover at American Colleges and Universities: Analysis of AAUP Data." *Economics of Education Review* 10(2): 99–110.

El-Khawas, Elaine H. 1989. *Campus Trends 1989.* Washington, D.C.: American Council on Education. ED 310 700. 84 pp. MF–01; PC–04.

———. 1991. "Senior Faculty in Academe: Active, Committed to the Teaching Role." *Research Briefs* 2(5). Washington, D.C.: American

Council on Education, Policy Analysis and Research.

Elmore, Charles J., and Robert T. Blackburn. 1983. "Black and White Faculty in White Research Universities." *Journal of Higher Education* 54(1): 1–15.

Exum, William H. 1983. "Climbing the Crystal Stair: Values, Affirmative Action, and Minority Faculty." *Social Problems* 30(4): 383–99.

Fairweather, James S. 1988. *Entrepreneurship and Higher Education: Lessons for Colleges, Universities, and Industry.* ASHE-ERIC Higher Education Report No. 6. Washington, D.C.: Association for the Study of Higher Education. ED 307 841. 88 pp. MF–01; PC–04.

———. 1992. "Teaching and the Faculty Reward Structure: Relationships between Faculty Activities and Compensation." Report of the National Center for Postsecondary Teaching, Learning, and Assessment. University Park: Pennsylvania State Univ.

Ferber, Marianne A. 1971. "Professors, Performance, and Rewards." *Industrial Relations* 13(1): 67–79.

Ferber, Marianne A., Jane W. Loeb, and Helen M. Lowry. 1978. "The Economic Status of Women Faculty: A Reappraisal." *Journal of Human Resources* 13(3): 385–401.

Finkelstein, M.O. 1980. "The Judicial Reception of Multiple Regression Studies in Race and Sex Discrimination Cases." *Columbia Law Review* 80: 737–54.

Finkelstein, Martin J. 1984a. *The American Academic Profession.* Columbus: Ohio State Univ. Press.

———. Spring 1984b. "The Status of Academic Women: An Assessment of Five Competing Explanations." *Review of Higher Education* 7: 223–46.

Flynn, Elizabeth A., John F. Flynn, Nancy Grimm, and Ted Lockhart. 1986. "The Part-time Problem: Four Voices." *Academe* 72(1): 12–18.

Folger, John, ed. 1984. *Financial Incentives for Academic Control.* New Directions for Higher Education No. 48. San Francisco: Jossey-Bass.

Fox, Mary Frank. 1981. "Sex, Salary, and Achievement: Reward-dualism in Academia." *Sociology of Education* 54(2): 71–84.

———. 1985. "Gender Segregation and Salary Structure in Academe." *Sociology of Work and Occupation* 8: 39–60.

Freeman, Richard B. 1975. "Supply and Salary Adjustments to the Changing Science Manpower Market: Physics, 1948–1973." *American Economic Review* 65(1): 27–39.

———. 1976. *The Overeducated American.* New York: Academic Press.

Gamson, Zelda F., Dorothy E. Finnegan, and Ted Il Koo Youn. 1990. "Assessing Faculty Shortages in Comprehensive Colleges and Universities." Working Paper No. 2. Boston: New England Resource Center for Higher Education. ED 351 899. 21 pp. MF–01; PC–01.

Gappa, Judith M. 1984. "Employing Part-time Faculty: Thoughtful

Approaches to Continuing Problems." *AAHE Bulletin* 37(2): 3–7. ED 254 134. 6 pp. MF–01; PC–01.

Gappa, Judith M., and David W. Leslie. 1993. *The Invisible Faculty: Improving the Status of Part-timers in Higher Education.* San Francisco: Jossey-Bass.

Goldstein, Michael B. 1987. "Equity Financing: Research Partnerships." In *Financing Higher Education: Strategies after Tax Reform,* edited by Richard E. Anderson and Joel W. Meyerson. New Directions for Higher Education No. 58. San Francisco: Jossey-Bass.

Gomez-Mejia, Luis R., and David B. Balkin. 1992. "Determinants of Faculty Pay: An Agency Theory Perspective." *Academy of Management Journal* 35(5): 921–55.

Gordon, Nancy M., Thomas E. Morton, and Ira C. Braden. 1974. "Faculty Salaries: Is There Discrimination by Sex, Race, and Discipline?" *American Economic Review* 64(3): 419–27.

Gray, Mary W. 1985. "Resisting Sex Discrimination against Faculty Women." *Academe* 71(5): 33–41.

Gray, Mary W., and Elizabeth L. Scott. May 1980. "A Statistical Remedy for Statistically Identified Discrimination." *Academe* 66: 174–81.

Gray, Peter J., Robert C. Froh, and Robert M. Diamond. 1991. "Myths and Realities." *AAHE Bulletin* 44(4): 4–7. ED 345 756. 4 pp. MF–01; PC–01.

Hacker, Andrew. 4 March 1992. "Too Many Professors: A Top-heavy Pyramid." *Chronicle of Higher Education* 38(26): B1–B2.

Hall, D.T. 1986. "Breaking Career Routines: Midcareer Choice and Identity." In *Career Development in Organizations,* edited by D.T. Hall and Associates. San Francisco: Jossey-Bass.

Hamermesh, Daniel S. 1988. "Salaries: Disciplinary Differences and Rank Injustices." *Academe* 74(3): 20–24.

Hamermesh, Daniel S., and Stephen A. Woodbury. 1991. "The Stagnant Fringe." *Academe* 77(3): 13–17.

Hansen, W. Lee. 1985. "Salary Differences across Disciplines." *Academe* 71(4): 6–7.

———. 1986. "Changes in Faculty Salaries." In *American Professors: A National Resource Imperiled,* edited by H.R. Bowen and J.H. Schuster. New York: Oxford Univ. Press.

———. 1988a. "Merit Pay in Higher Education." In *Academic Labor Markets and Careers in American Higher Education,* edited by David W. Breneman and Ted Il Koo Youn. New York: Falmer Press.

———. 1988b. "Merit Pay in Structured and Unstructured Salary Systems." *Academe* 74(6): 10–13.

Harvey, William B., and Dianne Scott-Jones. 1985. "We Can't Find Any: The Elusiveness of Black Faculty Members in American Higher Education." *Issues in Higher Education* 3(1): 68–76.

Haslinger, John A. June 1985. "Flexible Compensation: Getting a Return on Benefit Dollars." *Personnel Administrator:* 39–46.

Heller, Scott. 12 March 1986. "Colleges Permitting Employees to Tailor Fringe Benefits to Their Own Needs." *Chronicle of Higher Education* 32(31): 30–31.

Hendrickson, Robert M., and Barbara A. Lee. 1983. *Academic Employment and Retrenchment: Judicial Review and Administrative Action.* ASHE-ERIC Higher Education Report No. 8. Washington, D.C.: Association for the Study of Higher Education. ED 240 972. 83 pp. MF–01; PC–04.

Hoenack, Stephen A., et al. 1986. "The Marginal Costs of Instruction." *Research in Higher Education* 24(4): 335–470.

Hollenshead, Carol. 1992. "Faculty Women: Common Challenges, Different Strategies." Paper presented at a meeting of the National Association of Women in Education, San Antonio.

Horan, Patrick M. 1978. "Is Status Attainment Research Atheoretical?" *American Sociological Review* 43(4): 534–41.

Ikenberry, Stanley O. 1992. "The Decade Ahead." In *A Higher Education Map for the 1990s,* edited by Gene A. Budig. New York: ACE/Macmillan.

Johnson, George E., and Frank P. Stafford. 1974. "Lifelong Earnings in a Professional Labor Market: Academic Economists." *Journal of Political Economy* 82: 549–69.

———. 1979. "Pecuniary Rewards to Men and Women Faculty." In *Academic Rewards in Higher Education,* edited by Darrell R. Lewis and William E. Becker, Jr. Cambridge, Mass.: Ballenger Publishing Co.

Johnsrud, Linda K. 1992. "Barriers to Retention and Tenure: The Case of a University's Faculty Cohorts, 1982–1988." Paper presented at an annual meeting of the American Educational Research Association, San Francisco.

Justus, J.B., S.B. Freitag, and L.L. Parker. 1987. *The University of California in the Twenty-first Century: Successful Approaches to Faculty Diversity.* Berkeley: Univ. of California Press.

Kasper, Hirschel. 1986. "Finding the Merit in Merit Pay for Faculty." Unpublished paper. Oberlin College.

———. 1988. "Mastering the Academic Marketplace." *Academe* 74(2): 3–7.

Kastenbaum, Robert, and Caroline Schulte. 1988. "How Do Presidents of American Colleges and Universities Respond to the Prospect of Professors Who Cannot Be Forced to Retire?" Paper presented at a meeting of the Association for Gerontology in Higher Education, Chicago.

Katz, Daniel, and Robert Louis Kahn. 1978. *The Social Psychology of Organization.* New York: John Wiley & Sons.

Katz, David A. 1973. "Faculty Salaries, Promotions, and Productivity at a Large University." *American Economics Review* 63: 469–77.

Keister, Stephen D., and Lekha G. Keister. 1989. "Faculty Compensation and the Cost of Living in American Higher Education." *Journal of Higher Education* 60(4): 458–74.

Kellams, S.E., and Jay L. Chronister. 1987. "Life after Early Retirement: Faculty Activities and Perceptions." Paper presented at a meeting of the Association for the Study of Higher Education, Baltimore.

Keller, George. 1983. *Academic Strategy: The Management Revolution in American Higher Education.* Baltimore: Johns Hopkins Univ. Press.

Koch, James V., and John F. Chizmar, Jr. Fall 1973. "The Influence of Teaching and Other Factors upon Absolute Salaries and Salary Increments at Illinois State University." *Administrative Science Quarterly* 18: 27–34.

———. 1976. "Sex Discrimination and Affirmative Action in Faculty Salaries." *Economics Inquiry* 14(1): 16–23.

Konrad, Alison M., and Jeffrey Pfeffer. 1990. "Do You Get What You Deserve? Factors Affecting the Relationship between Productivity and Pay." *Administration Science Quarterly* 35(2): 258–85.

Kraft, Barbara S. 15 February 1984. "Day Care Programs Take Hold on Campuses." *Chronicle of Higher Education:* 21–22.

Langenburg, Donald N. 2 September 1992. "Team Scholarship Could Help Strengthen Scholarly Traditions." *Chronicle of Higher Education:* 64.

LaNoue, George R., and Barbara A. Lee. 1987. *Academics in Court: Consequences of Faculty Discrimination Litigation.* Ann Arbor: Univ. of Michigan Press.

Laury, M.M. 1988. "Contributing Factors in Career Advancement of Black Faculty Members at Traditionally White Institutions." Doctoral dissertation, Pennsylvania State Univ.

Lawler, Edward E. 1990. *Strategic Pay: Aligning Organizational Strategies and Pay Systems.* San Francisco: Jossey-Bass.

Lawrence, Janet H. 1985. "Developmental Needs as Intrinsic Incentives." In *Incentives for Faculty Vitality,* edited by Roger G. Baldwin. New Directions for Higher Education No. 51. San Francisco: Jossey-Bass.

Lawrence, Janet H., and Robert T. Blackburn. 1988. "Age as a Predictor of Faculty Productivity: Three Conceptual Approaches." *Journal of Higher Education* 59(1): 22–38.

Leap, Terry L. 1991. *Collective Bargaining and Labor Relations.* New York: Macmillan.

Lee, Barbara A. 1989. "Academic Personnel Policies and Practices: Managing the Process." In *Managing Faculty Resources,* edited by Gregory G. Lozier and Michael J. Dooris. New Directions for Institutional Research No. 63. San Francisco: Jossey-Bass.

Lee, Barbara A., David W. Leslie, and Steven G. Olswang. 1987. "Implications of Comparable Worth for Academe." *Journal of Higher Education* 58(6): 609–28.

Lee, Barbara A., and Steven G. Olswang. 1985. "Legal Parameters of the Faculty Employment Relationship." In *Higher Education: Handbook of Theory and Research,* edited by John C. Smart. New York: Agathon Press.

Leslie, David W. 1989. "Creative Staffing: Problems and Opportunities." In *Managing Faculty Resources,* edited by Gregory G. Lozier and Michael J. Dooris. New Directions for Institutional Research No. 63. San Francisco: Jossey-Bass.

Lester, Richard. 1974. *Antibias Regulations of Universities.* A report for the Carnegie Commission on Higher Education. New York: McGraw-Hill.

Levin, Henry M. 1991. "Raising Productivity in Higher Education." *Journal of Higher Education* 62(3): 162–241.

Lindgren, J. Ralph, Patti T. Ota, Perry A. Zirkel, and Nan Van Gieson. 1984. *Sex Discrimination Law in Higher Education: The Lessons of the Past Decade.* ASHE-ERIC Higher Education Report No. 4. Washington, D.C.: Association for the Study of Higher Education. ED 252 169. 86 pp. MF–01; PC–04.

Linnell, Robert H. 1979. "Age, Sex, and Ethnic Trade-offs in Faculty Employment: You Can't Have Your Cake and Eat It Too." *Current Issues in Higher Education* 4: 3–9.

Loeb, Jane W., Marianne A. Ferber, and Helen M. Lowry. 1978. "The Effectiveness of Affirmative Action for Women." *Journal of Higher Education* 49(3): 218–30.

Lohmann, Christopher K. 1991. "Retrenchment, Retirement Benefits, and the Faculty Role." *Academe* 77(3): 18–21.

Lozier, Gregory G., and Michael J. Dooris. 1987. "Is Higher Education Confronting Faculty Shortages?" Paper presented at a meeting of the Association for the Study of Higher Education, Baltimore. ED 292 386. 20 pp. MF–01; PC–01.

———. 1988–89. "Elimination of Mandatory Retirement: Anticipating Faculty Responses." *Planning for Higher Education* 17(2): 1–13.

McCaffery, Robert M. 1992. *Employee Benefit Programs: A Total Compensation Perspective.* 2d ed. Boston: PWS-KENT Publishing Co.

McElrath, Karen. 1992. "Gender, Career Disruption, and Academic Rewards." *Journal of Higher Education* 63(3): 269–81.

McGuire, Michael D., and Jane A. Price. 1989. "Faculty Replacement Needs for the Next 15 Years: A Simulated Attrition Model." Paper presented at a meeting of the Association for Institutional Research, Baltimore. ED 310 694. 39 pp. MF–01; PC–02.

McKeachie, Wilbert J. 1979. "Perspectives from Psychology: Financial Incentives Are Ineffective for Faculty." In *Academic Rewards in Higher Education,* edited by Darrell R. Lewis and William E. Becker, Jr. Cambridge, Mass.: Ballenger Publishing Co.

Mackey-Smith, A. 12 June 1984. "Large Shortage of Black Professors in Higher Education Grows Worse." *Wall Street Journal.*

Marchant, Gregory J., and Isadore Newman. 1991. "Faculty Evaluation and Reward Procedures: Views from Education Administrators." Paper presented at an annual conference of the American Educational Research Association, Chicago.

Marsh, Herbert W., and Kristine E. Dillon. 1980. "Academic Productivity and Faculty Supplemental Income." *Journal of Higher Education* 51(5): 546-55.

Marth, Edward C. 1988. "Merit Pay: Elm Street or Hollywood Boulevard?" *Academe* 74(6): 17-18.

Matier, Michael W. 1990. "Retaining Faculty: A Tale of Two Campuses." *Research in Higher Education* 30(1): 39-60.

Menges, Robert J., and William H. Exum. 1983. "Barriers to the Progress of Women and Minority Faculty." *Journal of Higher Education* 54(2): 123-44.

Milkovich, George T., and Jerry M. Newman. 1990. *Compensation.* Plano, Tex.: Business Publications.

Miller, Richard I. 1987. *Evaluating Faculty for Promotion and Tenure.* San Francisco: Jossey-Bass.

Mooney, Carolyn J. 2 August 1989. "Affirmative Action Goals, Coupled with Tiny Numbers of Minority Ph.D.s, Set Off Faculty Recruiting Frenzy." *Chronicle of Higher Education* 35(47).

———. 22 May 1991. "A Long-time Critic Crusades to Expose the Flaws of the Faculty-reward System." *Chronicle of Higher Education* 37(36).

Moore, Kathryn M., and Marilyn J. Amey. 1988. "Faculty Compensation: Making Sense of the Dollars." A report prepared for the National Education Association.

Moore, Kathryn M., and Michael P. Johnson. 1989. "The Status of Women and Minorities in the Professoriate: The Role of Affirmative Action and Equity." In *Managing Faculty Resources,* edited by Gregory G. Lozier and Michael J. Dooris. New Directions for Institutional Research No. 63. San Francisco: Jossey-Bass.

Moore, Kathryn M., and Mary Ann D. Sagaria. 1991. "The Situation of Women in Research Universities in the United States: Within the Circles of Academic Power." In *Women and Higher Education in Comparative Perspective,* edited by G.P. Kelley and S. Slaughter. Boston: Kluwer Academic Publishers.

Mortimer, Kenneth P., Marque Bagshaw, and Andrew T. Masland. 1985. *Flexibility in Academic Staffing: Effective Policies and Practices.* ASHE-ERIC Higher Education Report No. 1. Washington, D.C.: Association for the Study of Higher Education. ED 260 675. 121 pp. MF-01; PC-05.

Mott, Harold, and Arne Mjosland. 1989. "Chaos in Academia: The Salary Spectrum." *Journal of Educational Finance* 15(1): 67-83.

National Research Council. 1989. *Summary Report 1988: Doctorate Recipients for United State Universities.* Washington, D.C.: National

Academy Press.

Newman, Frank. 1979. "Can There Be Anything Affirmative about Affirmative Action in the '80s?" *Current Issues in Higher Education* 4: 15–18.

O'Briant, Walter H. 1991. "Professional Loyalty and the Scholarly Community: Reflections toward a Philosophy of Fostering Faculty." *Review of Higher Education* 14(2): 251–62.

Patten, Thomas Henry, Jr. 1988. *Fair Pay: The Managerial Challenge of Comparable Job Worth and Job Evaluation.* San Francisco: Jossey-Bass.

Pezzullo, Thomas R., and Barbara E. Brittingham. 1979. "The Assessment of Salary Equity: A Methodology, Alternatives, and a Dilemma." In *Salary Equity,* edited by Thomas R. Pezzullo and Barbara E. Brittingham. Lexington, Mass.: Lexington Books.

Pollack, J.S. 1986. "The Erosion of Tenure in the California State University." *Academe* 72(1): 19–24.

Pratt, Linda Ray. 1988. "Merit Pay: Reaganomics for the Faculty?" *Academe* 74(6): 14–16.

Reed, Rodney J. 1983. "Affirmative Action in Higher Education: Is It Necessary?" *Journal of Negro Education* 52(3): 332–49.

Remick, Helen. 1984. *Comparable Worth and Wages Discrimination: Technical Possibilities and Political Realities.* Philadelphia: Temple Univ. Press.

Reskin, Barbara, Deana Liddy, Lois Haiguere, and Lesley Lee Francis. July/August 1992. "Salary Setting Practices that Unfairly Disadvantage Women Faculty." *Academe:* 32–35.

Rice, R. Eugene. January 1986. "The Academic Profession in Transition: Toward a New Social Fiction. *Teaching Sociology* 14: 12–23.

Romero, Dan. 1977. "The Impact of and Use of Minority Faculty within a University." Paper presented at an annual meeting of the American Psychological Association, San Francisco. ED 146 240. 23 pp. MF–01; PC–01.

Rossman, Jack E. 1976. "Teaching, Publication, and Rewards at a Liberal Arts College." *Improving College and University Teaching* 24(4): 238–40.

Sacken, Donald M. 1990. "Taking Teaching Seriously: Institutional and Individual Dilemmas." *Journal of Higher Education* 61(5): 548–64.

Sandler, Bernice Resnick. 1979. "You've Come a Long Way, Maybe— Or Why It Still Hurts to Be a Woman in Labor." *Current Issues in Higher Education* 4: 11–14.

———. 29 February 1985. "The Quiet Revolution on Campus: How Sex Discrimination Has Changed." *Chronicle of Higher Education:* Back page.

Schein, Edgar M. 1980. *Organizational Psychology.* 3d ed. Englewood Cliffs, N.J.: Prentice-Hall.

Schoenfeld, Clay. 1992. "Answering the Big Question: When Should I Retire?" *AAHE Bulletin* 44(9): 11–13.

Schuster, Jack H. 1990. "Faculty Issues in the 1990s: New Realities, New Opportunities." In *An Agenda for the New Decade,* edited by Larry W. Jones and Frank A. Nowotny. New Directions for Higher Education No. 70. San Francisco: Jossey-Bass.

Schuster, Jack H., Daniel W. Wheeler, and Associates, eds. 1990. *Enhancing Faculty Careers: Strategies for Development and Renewal.* San Francisco: Jossey-Bass.

Seldin, Peter. 1990. "Academic Environments and Teaching Effectiveness." In *How Administrators Can Improve Teaching,* edited by Peter Seldin and Associates. San Francisco: Jossey-Bass.

Silander, Fred. 1983. "Faculty Compensation Issues." In *Issues in Faculty Personnel Policies,* edited by Jon W. Fuller. New Directions for Higher Education No. 41. San Francisco: Jossey-Bass.

Smart, John S. 1991. "Gender Equity in Academic Rank and Salary." *Review of Higher Education* 14(1): 511–26.

Smelser, Neal J., and R. Content. 1980. *The Changing Academic Labor Market: General Trends and a Berkeley Case Study.* Berkeley: Univ. of California Press.

Smith, Earl, and Stephanie L. Witt. 1990. "Black Faculty and Affirmative Action at Predominantly White Institutions." *Western Journal of Black Studies* 14(1): 9–16.

Snyder, Julie K., Gerald W. McLaughlin, and James R. Montgomery. 1992. "Diagnosing and Dealing with Salary Compression." *Research in Higher Education* 33(1): 113–24.

Sorcinelli, Mary Deana. 1988. "Satisfaction, Stress High for New Faculty." *Campus Report: Indiana State University–Bloomington* 11: 1–4.

Spector, J.D. December 1989. "The Minnesota Plan II." Minneapolis: Univ. of Minnesota.

Strategic Study Group on the Status of Women. 1988. "Report to the President and the Commission for Women." Recommendation Package No. 5. University Park: Pennsylvania State Univ., Office of Planning and Analysis. ED 319 303. 161 pp. MF–01; PC–07.

Szafran, Robert F. 1984. *Universities and Women Faculty: Why Some Organizations Discriminate More Than Others.* New York: Praeger.

Tucker, Charles W. 1987. "Academic 'Stars' and Faculty Responsibility." *Academe* 73(3): 10–11.

Tuckman, Barbara H. 1979. "Salary Differences among University Faculty and Their Implications for the Future." In *Salary Equity: Detecting Sex Bias in Salaries among College and University Professors,* edited by Thomas R. Pezzullo and Barbara E. Brittingham. Lexington, Mass.: D.C. Heath & Co.

Tuckman, Barbara H., and Howard P. Tuckman. 1976. "The Structure of Salaries at American Universities." *Journal of Higher Education*

47(1): 51–64.

———. 1980. "Part-timers, Sex Discrimination, and Career Choice at Two-year Institutions." *Academe* 66: 71–76.

Tuckman, Howard P. 1976. *Publication, Teaching, and the Academic Reward Structure.* Lexington, Mass.: Lexington Books.

———. 1979. "The Academic Reward Structure in American Higher Education." In *Academic Rewards in Higher Education,* edited by Darrell R. Lewis and William E. Becker, Jr. Cambridge, Mass.: Ballenger Publishing Co.

———. 1987. "The Academic Reward Structure in American Higher Education." In *The American Academic Profession,* edited by Martin J. Finkelstein. Columbus: Ohio State Univ. Press.

Tuckman, Howard P., and M. Belisle. 1987. "The Career Status of New Doctorates One or Two Years Later." *Educational Record* 68(1): 32–35.

Tuckman, Howard P., and Kane L. Pickerill. 1988. "Part-time Faculty and Part-time Academic Careers." In *Academic Labor Markets and Careers,* edited by David W. Breneman and Ted I.K. Youn. New York: Falmer Press.

U.S. Dept. of Education. 1987. *College Faculty Salaries, 1976–86.* Washington, D.C.: Office of Educational Research and Improvement. ED 286 413. 19 pp. MF–01; PC–01.

Univ. of Kansas. 1990. *College Guidelines on Counter Offers.* Lawrence: Univ. of Kansas, College of Liberal Arts and Sciences, Office of the Dean.

———. 1991. *KanElect: Your Dependent Care Flexible Spending Account.* Lawrence: Univ. of Kansas, Div. of Personnel Services, Dept. of Administration.

Waggamon, John S. 1983. *Faculty Recruitment, Retention, and Fair Employment: Obligations and Opportunities.* ASHE-ERIC Higher Education Report No. 2. Washington, D.C.: Association for the Study of Higher Education. ED 227 806. 73 pp. MF–01; PC–03.

Warner, Timothy R. Spring 1988. "College Costs: A View from a Private University." *College Board Review* 147: 16–19+.

Washington, Valora, and William Harvey. 1989. *Affirmative Rhetoric, Negative Action: African-American and Hispanic Faculty in Predominantly White Institutions.* ASHE-ERIC Higher Education Report No. 2. Washington, D.C.: Association for the Study of Higher Education. ED 316 075. 128 pp. MF–01; PC–06.

Weiler, William C. 1985. "Why Do Faculty Members Leave a University?" *Research in Higher Education* 23(3): 270–77.

Wheeler, Daniel W., and Jack H. Schuster. 1990. "Building Comprehensive Programs to Enhance Faculty Development." In *Enhancing Faculty Careers: Strategies for Development and Renewal,* edited by Jack H. Schuster, Daniel W. Wheeler, and Associates. San Francisco: Jossey-Bass.

White, Charles S. 1990. "Salary and Gender Discrimination Is a Public Institution." *CUPA Journal* 41(4): 17–25.

Whitt, Elizabeth J. 1991. "Hit the Ground Running: Experiences of New Faculty in a School of Education." *Review of Higher Education* 14(2): 177–98.

Wilson, Reginald. 1987. "Recruitment and Retention of Minority Faculty and Staff." *AAHE Bulletin* 39(6): 11–14.

Witt, Stephanie L., and Nicholas P. Lovrich. 1988. "Sources of Stress among Faculty: Gender Differences." *Review of Higher Education* 11(3): 269–84.

Woloshin, Phyllis. 1986. "If You're So Smart, Why Aren't You Rich?" In *Controversies and Decisions in Hard Economic Times,* edited by Billie Wright Dziech. New Directions for Community Colleges No. 53. San Francisco: Jossey-Bass.

Youn, Ted Il Koo. 1988. "Studies of Academic Markets and Careers: An Historical Review." In *Academic Labor Markets and Careers,* edited by David W. Breneman and Ted Il Koo Youn. New York: Falmer Press.

Youn, Ted Il Koo, and Daniel Zelterman. 1988. "Institutional Career Mobility in Academia." In *Academic Labor Markets and Careers,* edited by David W. Breneman and Ted Il Koo Youn. New York: Falmer Press.

Yuker, Harold E. 1984. *Faculty Workload: Research, Theory, and Interpretation.* ASHE-ERIC Higher Education Report No. 10. Washington, D.C.: Association for the Study of Higher Education. ED 259 691. 120 pp. MF–01; PC 05.

Zenger, Todd R. 1992. "Why Do Employers Only Reward Extreme Performance? Examining the Relationships among Performance, Pay, and Turnover." *Administrative Science Quarterly* 37(2): 198–219.

INDEX

A

AAUP. *See* American Association of University Professors
"absorbing errand," 32
academic discipline and sex, relationship between, 69
academic labor markets multiple and mission dependent, 15
academics, decline in salary, 19-20
affirmative action
       mandated, 59
       results, 73
       strategic initiatives, 86
"affirmative defenses," 67
African-American faculty, 74, 75
Age Discrimination in Employment Act of 1967, 59-60, 75
age discrimination in salaries, 76
American Association of Higher Education, 39
American Association of University Professors (AAUP), 19, 87
       salary reports, 43
American Educational Research Association, 39
American Federation of State, County, and
   Municipal Employees, 72
Amey, Marilyn J., xvi
annuity factor in merit pay, 88
appointment, two people sharing, 24

B

base pay, determination of 10-11
Base salary, 1
base salary and benefits, relationships between, 6-7
benefits program, role in strategic compensation, 11-12
benefits, growing demand for new programs, 52
Braskamp, David, xvii
Brocato, Joe, xvii
Brown (1965), 8
burnout, 27
business, discipline of, 43

C

"cafeteria-style," benefits. *See* flexible benefits
causal modeling, 71
Center for the Study of Higher Education, xvii
child care, growing interest in benefit of, 5·
City University of New York, 70
Civil Rights Act of 1964, Title VII, 59, 60, 66
class action suits, 70
clinical appointments, 24
collective bargaining, 6, 13, 15, 85
       alternative to multidisciplinary markets, 22-24
       provide degree of stabilization, 23

Executive Order
        11246, 59
        11375, 59
external equity, 11
extra compensation source, additional teaching is, 54

F

Faculty Job Satisfaction: Women and Minorities in Peril, xv
faculty
        compensation criteria, 7
        development and renewal programs, 46
        fee-for-service, growing societal mistrust for, 55
        morale, level of compensation determinant of, 32
        pool, generating a prospective, 18
        rank as definition of compensation policies, 42
        reward structures, 8, 47-49
        salaries, improvement more apparent than real, 19-20
        stars, recruitment of, 53
        within a multidisciplinary market, 21-22
Fair Labor Standards Act of 1938, 59
Fairweather, Dr. James, xvii
family care initiatives for faculty, 5
fields, very market-driven seem to emphasize teaching, 40
flagging, 69-70
flexible benefits, 4
forecasting labor market, 26
Freeman (1975), 8
fringe benefits, 2-4
Galton's Paradox, 63

G

gay men, spousal benefits, 5-6
gender
        and ethnicity compensation determinants, 34
        as a predictor variable, 71
        indirectly influences salary, variables through 71
gender-neutral benefits, pressure growing to provide, 73
graduate students, increase in indebtedness, 20-21

H

Health, Education and Welfare, Department of, 59
Hispanics in higher education, 74, 75
human capital
        framework, 8, 71
        theory, 62-64

I

importance of nonmonetary factors, study on, 50

The Costs and Uses of Faculty Compensation

incentives for early retirement, 25-28
income, supplemental, 54
indirect compensation. *See* fringe benefits
indispensable, openness about pay for performance, 39
informal merit-based ethos, usually exists, 39
institutional
      compensation for off campus activities of staff, 55
      reward structure, perceived differently throughout
            career, 46
internal equity, 11
inverted professorial pyramid, 45

K

"knowledge-work" organization, 8

L

labor market, influence on salaries, 45
Lawler, 10
lesbians, spousal benefits, 5-6

M

market position, 11
maternity and parental leaves, need increases, 5
merit pay, 34-39
      depends upon a variety of factors, 67
      difficulties in using, 35-38
      does it actually work?, 36-38
      removal of, 23
      total compensation usually unrelated to performance, 37
Michigan State University, xvi, xvii
"mission statements," 10
models of supply and demand, various, 8
Montana State University, 70
Moore, Kathryn M., xvi, xvii

N

National
      Center for Educational Statistics, 61
      Survey of Postsecondary Education Faculty, 61, 74
need, criteria of, 7
negative
      relationship between undergraduate teaching
         & compensation, 41
      tenure slope, for salary, 45, 78
new programs and services for women, 73
nonmonetary benefits, 32-33

sabbatical programs, 46
salaries, largest single element in budget, 49
Salary Equity, 68
"salary dispersion," 78
salary. *See also* pay
    compression, definition of, 77-78
    discrimination, methods to establish statistically, 67
    discrimination, studies mostly concern gender, 60
    variable that might affect determination of, 8
senior faculty decisions to leave an institution, study of, 51
sex discrimination
    cases, 66, 78-79
    compensation prohibition, 59
Smart (1991), 71
sound pay system, basic qualities of, 80
standards of performance, need to establish, 35
starting salaries as benchmarks for determining base salaries, 2
strategic compensation, 10
strategic pay, 9
    Lawyer's idea of, 38
structural functionalism, 71
structuring compensation, 10-12
study leaves of absence, 46
supply and demand [theory], 64-65
systems of reward (compensation), 31

T
Tack, Martha and Carol Pattitu, xv
teaching
    assignments, variation in, 46
    inverse relationship with institutional reward
      structures, 40
    orientation increases effect of salary on staff, 50
    rewarded far less, 49
    undergraduates not rewarded by institutional
      structures, 42
tenure denial, study on, 50
"threshold issue," 66
Tuckman, 8, 9

U
"underutilization," 65
United States Supreme Court, 60, 71
universities tend to fund individuals rather than positions, 44
University of Kansas, xvi
    College of Liberal Arts and Sciences, 52-53
University of Michigan, 5, 62
University of Minnesota, 70

ASHE-ERIC HIGHER EDUCATION REPORTS

Since 1983, the Association for the Study of Higher Education (ASHE) and the Educational Resources Information Center (ERIC) Clearinghouse on Higher Education, a sponsored project of the School of Education and Human Development at The George Washington University, have cosponsored the *ASHE-ERIC Higher Education Report* series. The 1993 series is the twenty-second overall and the fifth to be published by the School of Education and Human Development at the George Washington University.

Each monograph is the definitive analysis of a tough higher education problem, based on thorough research of pertinent literature and institutional experiences. Topics are identified by a national survey. Noted practitioners and scholars are then commissioned to write the reports, with experts providing critical reviews of each manuscript before publication.

Eight monographs (10 before 1985) in the ASHE-ERIC Higher Education Report series are published each year and are available on individual and subscription bases. Subscription to eight issues is $98.00 annually; $78 to members of AAHE, AIR, or AERA; and $68 to ASHE members. All foreign subscribers must include an additional $10 per series year for postage.

To order, use the order form on the last page of this book. Regular prices are as follows:

Series	Price	Series	Price
1993	$18.00	1985 to 87	$10.00
1990 to 92	$17.00	1983 and 84	$7.50
1988 and 89	$15.00	before 1983	$6.50

Discounts on non-subscription orders:
* Bookstores, and current members of AERA, AIR, AAHE and ASHE, receive a 25% discount.
* Bulk: For non-bookstore, non-member orders of 10 or more books, deduct 10%.

Shipping costs are as follows:
* U.S. address: 5% of invoice subtotal for orders over $50.00; $2.50 for each order with an invoice subtotal of $50.00 or less.
* Foreign: $2.50 per book.
  All orders under $45.00 must be prepaid. Make check payable to ASHE-ERIC. For Visa or MasterCard, include card number, expiration date and signature.

Address order to
ASHE-ERIC Higher Education Reports
The George Washington University
1 Dupont Circle, Suite 630
Washington, DC 20036
Or phone (202) 296-2597
Write or call for a complete catalog.

1993 ASHE-ERIC Higher Education Reports

1. The Department Chair: New Roles, Responsibilities and Challenges
   Alan T. Seagren, John W. Creswell, and Daniel W. Wheeler

2. Sexual Harassment in Higher Education: From Conflict to Community
   Robert O. Riggs, Patricia H. Murrell, and JoAnn C. Cutting

3. Chicanos in Higher Education: Issues and Dilemmas for the 21st Century
   by Adalberto Aguirre, Jr., and Ruben O. Martinez

4. Academic Freedom in American Higher Education: Rights, Responsibilities, and Limitations
   by Robert K. Poch

1992 ASHE-ERIC Higher Education Reports

1. The Leadership Compass: Values and Ethics in Higher Education
   John R. Wilcox and Susan L. Ebbs

2. Preparing for a Global Community: Achieving an International Perspective in Higher Education
   Sarah M. Pickert

3. Quality: Transforming Postsecondary Education
   Ellen Earle Chaffee and Lawrence A. Sherr

4. Faculty Job Satisfaction: Women and Minorities in Peril
   Martha Wingard Tack and Carol Logan Patitu

5. Reconciling Rights and Responsibilities of Colleges and Students: Offensive Speech, Assembly, Drug Testing, and Safety
   Annette Gibbs

6. Creating Distinctiveness: Lessons from Uncommon Colleges and Universities
   Barbara K. Townsend, L. Jackson Newell, and Michael D. Wiese

7. Instituting Enduring Innovations: Achieving Continuity of Change in Higher Education
   Barbara K. Curry

8. Crossing Pedagogical Oceans: International Teaching Assistants in U.S. Undergraduate Education
   Rosslyn M. Smith, Patricia Byrd, Gayle L. Nelson, Ralph Pat Barrett, and Janet C. Constantinides

1991 ASHE-ERIC Higher Education Reports

1. Active Learning: Creating Excitement in the Classroom
   Charles C. Bonwell and James A. Eison

2. Realizing Gender Equality in Higher Education: The Need to Integrate Work/Family Issues
   Nancy Hensel

3. Academic Advising for Student Success: A System of Shared Responsibility
   Susan H. Frost

4. Cooperative Learning: Increasing College Faculty Instructional Productivity
   David W. Johnson, Roger T. Johnson, and Karl A. Smith

5. High School–College Partnerships: Conceptual Models, Programs, and Issues
   Arthur Richard Greenberg

6. Meeting the Mandate: Renewing the College and Departmental Curriculum
   William Toombs and William Tierney

7. Faculty Collaboration: Enhancing the Quality of Scholarship and Teaching
   Ann E. Austin and Roger G. Baldwin

8. Strategies and Consequences: Managing the Costs in Higher Education
   John S. Waggaman

1990 ASHE-ERIC Higher Education Reports

1. The Campus Green: Fund Raising in Higher Education
   Barbara E. Brittingham and Thomas R. Pezzullo

2. The Emeritus Professor: Old Rank - New Meaning
   James E. Mauch, Jack W. Birch, and Jack Matthews

3. "High Risk" Students in Higher Education: Future Trends
   Dionne J. Jones and Betty Collier Watson

4. Budgeting for Higher Education at the State Level: Enigma, Paradox, and Ritual
   Daniel T. Layzell and Jan W. Lyddon

5. Proprietary Schools: Programs, Policies, and Prospects
   John B. Lee and Jamie P. Merisotis

6. College Choice: Understanding Student Enrollment Behavior
   Michael B. Paulsen

7. Pursuing Diversity: Recruiting College Minority Students
   Barbara Astone and Elsa Nuñez-Wormack

8. Social Consciousness and Career Awareness: Emerging Link in Higher Education
   John S. Swift, Jr.

1989 ASHE-ERIC Higher Education Reports

1. Making Sense of Administrative Leadership: The 'L' Word in Higher Education
   Estela M. Bensimon, Anna Neumann, and Robert Birnbaum

2. Affirmative Rhetoric, Negative Action: African-American and Hispanic Faculty at Predominantly White Universities
   Valora Washington and William Harvey

3. Postsecondary Developmental Programs: A Traditional Agenda with New Imperatives
   Louise M. Tomlinson

4. The Old College Try: Balancing Athletics and Academics in Higher Education
   John R. Thelin and Lawrence L. Wiseman

5. The Challenge of Diversity: Involvement or Alienation in the Academy?
   Daryl G. Smith

6. Student Goals for College and Courses: A Missing Link in Assessing and Improving Academic Achievement
   Joan S. Stark, Kathleen M. Shaw, and Malcolm A. Lowther

7. The Student as Commuter: Developing a Comprehensive Institutional Response
   Barbara Jacoby

8. Renewing Civic Capacity: Preparing College Students for Service and Citizenship
   Suzanne W. Morse

1988 ASHE-ERIC Higher Education Reports

1. The Invisible Tapestry: Culture in American Colleges and Universities
   George D. Kuh and Elizabeth J. Whitt

2. Critical Thinking: Theory, Research, Practice, and Possibilities
   Joanne Gainen Kurfiss

3. Developing Academic Programs: The Climate for Innovation
   Daniel T. Seymour

4. Peer Teaching: To Teach is To Learn Twice
   Neal A. Whitman

5. Higher Education and State Governments: Renewed Partnership, Cooperation, or Competition?
   Edward R. Hines

6. Entrepreneurship and Higher Education: Lessons for Colleges, Universities, and Industry
   James S. Fairweather

7. Planning for Microcomputers in Higher Education: Strategies for the Next Generation
   Reynolds Ferrante, John Hayman, Mary Susan Carlson, and Harry Phillips

8. The Challenge for Research in Higher Education: Harmonizing Excellence and Utility
   Alan W. Lindsay and Ruth T. Neumann

1987 ASHE-ERIC Higher Education Reports

1. Incentive Early Retirement Programs for Faculty: Innovative Responses to a Changing Environment
   Jay L. Chronister and Thomas R. Kepple, Jr.

2. Working Effectively with Trustees: Building Cooperative Campus Leadership
   Barbara E. Taylor

3. Formal Recognition of Employer-Sponsored Instruction: Conflict and Collegiality in Postsecondary Education
   Nancy S. Nash and Elizabeth M. Hawthorne

4. Learning Styles: Implications for Improving Educational Practices
   Charles S. Claxton and Patricia H. Murrell

5. Higher Education Leadership: Enhancing Skills through Professional Development Programs
   Sharon A. McDade

6. Higher Education and the Public Trust: Improving Stature in Colleges and Universities
   Richard L. Alfred and Julie Weissman

7. College Student Outcomes Assessment: A Talent Development Perspective
   Maryann Jacobi, Alexander Astin, and Frank Ayala, Jr.

8. Opportunity from Strength: Strategic Planning Clarified with Case Examples
   Robert G. Cope

1986 ASHE-ERIC Higher Education Reports

1. Post-tenure Faculty Evaluation: Threat or Opportunity?
   Christine M. Licata

2. Blue Ribbon Commissions and Higher Education: Changing Academe from the Outside
   Janet R. Johnson and Laurence R. Marcus

3. Responsive Professional Education: Balancing Outcomes and Opportunities
   Joan S. Stark, Malcolm A. Lowther, and Bonnie M.K. Hagerty

4. Increasing Students' Learning: A Faculty Guide to Reducing Stress among Students
   Neal A. Whitman, David C. Spendlove, and Claire H. Clark

5. Student Financial Aid and Women: Equity Dilemma?
   Mary Moran

6. The Master's Degree: Tradition, Diversity, Innovation
   Judith S. Glazer

7. The College, the Constitution, and the Consumer Student: Implications for Policy and Practice
   Robert M. Hendrickson and Annette Gibbs

8. Selecting College and University Personnel: The Quest and the Question
   Richard A. Kaplowitz

1985 ASHE-ERIC Higher Education Reports

1. Flexibility in Academic Staffing: Effective Policies and Practices
   Kenneth P. Mortimer, Marque Bagshaw, and Andrew T. Masland

2. Associations in Action: The Washington, D.C. Higher Education Community
   Harland G. Bloland

3. And on the Seventh Day: Faculty Consulting and Supplemental Income
   Carol M. Boyer and Darrell R. Lewis

4. Faculty Research Performance: Lessons from the Sciences and Social Sciences
   John W. Creswell

5. Academic Program Review: Institutional Approaches, Expectations, and Controversies
   Clifton F. Conrad and Richard F. Wilson

6. Students in Urban Settings: Achieving the Baccalaureate Degree
   Richard C. Richardson, Jr. and Louis W. Bender

7. Serving More Than Students: A Critical Need for College Student Personnel Services
   Peter H. Garland

8. Faculty Participation in Decision Making: Necessity or Luxury?
   Carol E. Floyd

*Out-of-print. Available through EDRS. Call 1-800-443-ERIC.

ORDER FORM

Quantity   **Amount**

_____ Please begin my subscription to the 1993 *ASHE-ERIC Higher Education Reports* at $98.00, 32% off the cover price, starting with Report 1, 1993.   _____

_____ Please send a complete set of the 1992 *ASHE-ERIC Higher Education Reports* at $90.00, 33% off the cover price.   _____

_____ Outside the U.S., add $10.00 per series for postage.   _____

Individual reports are avilable at the following prices:

1993, $18.00	1985 to 1987, $10.00
1990 to 1992, $17.00	1983 and 1984, $7.50
1988 and 1989, $15.00	1980 to 1982, $6.50

SHIPPING: **U.S. Orders:** *For subtotal (before discount) of $50.00 or less, add $2.50. For subtotal over $50.00, add 5% of subtotal. Call for rush service options.* **Foreign Orders:** *$2.50 per book.* **U.S. Subscriptions:** *Included in price.* **Foreign Subscriptions:** *Add $10.00.*

PLEASE SEND ME THE FOLLOWING REPORTS:

Quantity	Report No.	Year	Title	Amount

Subtotal:	
Shipping:	
Total Due:	

Please check one of the following:
☐ Check enclosed, payable to GWU–ERIC.
☐ Purchase order attached ($45.00 minimum).
☐ Charge my credit card indicated below:
    ☐ Visa   ☐ MasterCard

Expiration Date _____

Name _____

Title _____

Institution _____

Address _____

City _____ State _____ Zip _____

Phone _____ Fax _____ Telex _____

Signature _____ Date _____

SEND ALL ORDERS TO:
ASHE-ERIC Higher Education Reports
The George Washington University
One Dupont Circle, Suite 630
Washington, DC 20036-1183
Phone: (202) 296-2597